101
Silly Stories from Cheerful China
—— China Daily Hotpot Column Collection

The front cover features major contributors to the book: (clockwise) Erik Nilsson, Stuart Beaton, Xie Fang, Patrick Whiteley, Thomas Talhelm, Liu Jun, Jane Hanson and Sandra Lee.

图书在版编目（ＣＩＰ）数据

文化火锅：英文／中国日报特稿部编. —北京：五洲传播
出版社,2010.8
ISBN 978-7-5085-1863-3

Ⅰ.①文…　　Ⅱ.①中…　　Ⅲ.①比较文化－中国、外
国－文集－英文　　Ⅳ.①G04-53

中国版本图书馆CIP数据核字（2010）第141543号

文化火锅

出版发行：五洲传播出版社

编　　者：刘　浚　　　　　　校　　读：Erik Nilsson
责任编辑：郑　磊　　　　　　装帧设计：缪　惟／杜　宇

社址：北京市海淀区北三环中路31号生产力大楼B座7层
邮政编码：100088
发行电话：010-82005927，010-82007837

网址：http://www.cicc.org.cn

制版单位：北京锦绣圣艺文化发展有限公司

开本：787×1092　　1/16　　　　　印张：17

ISBN 978-7-5085-1863-3　　　　　定价：99.00元

Acknowledgements

To all the contributors who have shared their wonderful experiences with China Daily's readers.

To Ji Tao, Raymond Zhou, Erik Nilsson, Patrick Whiteley, and many others who have written stories and helped uphold the level of the Hotpot column.

Preface

"Why did you cut the punch line, 'Revenge is a dish best served cold'?" asked Australian Patrick Whiteley, a former China Daily editor. I replied: "I just thought cold dishes are delicious, and why shouldn't anyone like them?" Exasperated, he explained, "But in the West, 'revenge is a dish served cold' means to treat someone badly in retaliation."

Oops.

It's not an easy job to be the editor of China Daily's "Hotpot" column. After taking the charge to keep the column alive and kicking in January 2007, I've learned there are many barrier reefs beneath the seemingly placid surface of the sea of English-language writing about China.

As the national English-language newspaper, China Daily has undertaken slews of reforms to engage its readership over the years. From Tuesday to Thursday for several years, the Hotpots have regularly appeared on China Daily's page 20.

While the Hotpot column was designed to allow any good writing to be thrown into the soup — much like various tasty tidbits are tossed into the bubbling cauldron that is real hotpot — conflicting views among editors made some guidelines necessary. They should not be merely a statement of facts but, rather, ought to be written in witty, quirky and descriptive ways. Unlike the editorials in the opinion section, Hotpots should be personal — amusing experiences or thought-provoking observations of human nature and reality. The column should never offend nor poke fun at the weak and disadvantaged.

This collection features 101 of the best Hotpots among the hundreds published over the years. While many authors discussed their first impressions of transportation, shopping and traveling in this country, some also pondered cultural differences through marvelous writing riddled with rich and vivid examples. Browsing through the book, one will get the firsthand accounts of different cultural perspectives from dozens of contributors from various corners and folds of the globe.

While sorting through stories for this collection, I came to realize that love, weddings and marriage seem to be a favorite theme. American Erik Nilsson, a quiet young man whose stories never failed to get a guffaw from us, has actually "married" — yet never "divorced" — a number of girls from various ethnic groups during his journeys throughout the country. During Christmas in 2009, he limped around the capital in a Santa suit with a fractured foot along with dozens of other Kris Kringles. While the story made me cry from laughing so hard, everyone in the office thought dear Erik truly needed a break. What a surprise it was then to read his next Hotpot that on New Year's Day, he had hobbled on crutches cut from saplings along a cliff into a mountain-locked village in Yunnan province.

China might seem a vast, mysterious Middle Kingdom that's overwhelming for first-time visitors. But as many of our authors have discovered, the minute one decides to walk out of the safe zone to embrace the unknown, new adventures with wonderful and weird people abound.

And as the "dish served cold" versus "cold dish" incident illustrates, there's so much more to learn about a culture than its language. People must learn to respect others, especially those from different backgrounds, before real understanding and communication can be possible. Perhaps China Daily's Hotpot serves as a melting pot in which our thoughts and actions boil over, enabling all of us to share our different tastes for the spice of life.

I am grateful to all the authors who have taken my suggestions seriously and rewritten their fine stories up to five or six times before this picky editor would give them the thumbs up. If you want to contribute — and are willing to put up with the fastidious editor's endless suggestions — please drop us a line or two to hotpot@chinadaily.com.cn.

Liu Jun
Hotpot column editor
China Daily

CONTENTS

I. GENERALLY SPEAKING

II. Culture vultures

I. GENERALLY SPEAKING

1. CLOSE ENCOUNTERS OF THE WEIRD KIND

1. CEO soaks it in

This lighting manufacturer was hoping to make a big splash with its environmental campaign to adopt three giant pandas and make them mascots of climate-change awareness — and got a lot more than it bargained for.

The press conference was meant to be their show, but it was the Wolong Reserve park staffers who really poured it on — that is, by accidentally dumping gallons of pooled rainwater all over the company's CEO during his speech.

Despite the rainfall that has been sheeting down upon Sichuan province over the past few weeks, the media-savvy PR firm decided to hold the conference under a canopy pitched in front of the living habitat of the to-be-adopted pandas. This ensured the press could get an eye-full of the cuddly critters as they frolicked and nibbled bamboo, while government and park officials inked the adoption agreement with the CEO.

However, the canopy roof was fashioned from a tarp stretched across a flat roof frame, so that the downpour — rather than running off the roof's sides — pooled in the pockets between the grid of crossbeams.

Suddenly, all eyes were cast towards the roof, which was now a checkerboard of concave squares, in each of which the weight of the accumulated water was causing the canopy to droop.

One park staffer decided to take action and took up a long bamboo fishnet, which for some reason was pointed on the end not used to scoop aquatic creatures from deep waters.

But rather than pushing the water up and out over the edge with the netted end, he punctured the canopy — to the English-language protests of the CEO, who yelled: "No! No! Use the other end!"

Audience members snatched up their electronic gizmos and bags and scuttled away from him in the nick of time, effectively evading the cascade.

With all participants still high and dry, things returned to normalcy. Predictable and scripted speeches proceeded as reporters furiously scribbled in their notebooks.

Then, with a sudden popping sound, the sharpened tip of the bamboo shaft ruptured downwards through another sagging square of roof from above. Unsuspecting audience members again fled to keep from getting soaked.

Apparently, a park staffer had crawled on the roof to take a stab at removing the excess water. A faint shadow could be seen from below as he stalked to and fro atop the structure, until the ominous dark spot came to pause over the square directly above the stage where the VIPs sat at a dressed-up table. The CEO had just enough time — a millisecond, it seemed — to look up and realize he was about to be hosed.

Another popping rip announced the puncture of the tarp, and gravity took its course. A small but torrential cascade splooshed down atop his head, and calamity erupted among the onlookers.

Astonishment faded into laughter, and there stood the soaked CEO.

But he was determined not to let the drenching dampen his spirits, and after a few guffaws, he burst into a hearty round of *Singing in the Rain*.

I'm willing to bet that when this company decided to stage this event to expound their concern for climate problems, this wasn't exactly one they had in mind.

ERIK NILSSON
(July 31, 2007)

2. Dealing with the Devils

One of them grabbed my arms, and another seized my legs.

Then, these musclemen effortlessly picked me up and lobbed me into the back of a nearby cab.

"You," they said, "are coming with us!"

My protests fell on deaf ears. I was being shanghaied in Beijing.

I had been out all night researching a story about the capital's night-lifers. Beijing, it seems, is a massive metropolis with an early bedtime. But we wanted to know about its night owls who don't give two hoots about getting the worm.

So, naturally, I approached the brawny bunch I saw swigging celebratory beer from a trophy on Gongtibeilu just before sunrise.

I wondered what this rowdy rugby team was doing. Little did I know I was dealing with the Beijing Devils. And when I found out, all hell broke loose.

Before I could even introduce myself, these hellions howled: "He's a reporter! Let's get him!"

And then they did.

I still have no idea what the devil possessed them to go through with their hellish abduction scheme. But I did learn that the night began with 32 teammates making good use of their half-price discount at The Den. By this point, only eight Devils were still raising hell. The last men standing boasted of having guzzled about 15 pints topped off with four to five shots apiece.

That could explain why one of my kidnappers, who I later learned was a Welshman named Samuel John Lockyer, pulled a stunt jump and roll from the window of our taxi. This seriously confounded our cabbie, whose confusion compounded when Lockyer reentered through the other passenger door a few seconds later.

"I don't know them. Really," I told the driver in Chinese.

Once the remaining team members had coordinated a taxi caravan, they were off to the Goose and Duck sports pub, equipment and captive reporter in tow.

Apparently, the job of a journalist who has been nabbed by a rugby team isn't getting usable quotes. At least, that seemed to be reflected by the uncooperative attitude of my captors. Nor is it to pull in a handsome ransom.Instead, his job is being force-fed copious amounts of beer from the team's most recently won trophy — in this case, hailing from a 10-0 trouncing of the Beijing Aardvarks.

"The sweet taste of victory," roared Lockyer, as he pressed the bottom lip of the trophy firmly against the bottom lip of my face.

As the sweet taste of victory spilled down my throat — and shirtfront — I began planning my escape.

But as the sun poked over the horizon, the Devils seemed to pull in their horns and became preoccupied with dancing and mock sword fighting with the pool sticks.

I grabbed my notebook, which my captors had scribbled with various profanities and obscene doodles during a game of keep-away, and headed for the door.

Once safely outside, I turned to wave goodbye to my captors, who bellowed out several farewells to "Spiderman", which was the name they used to refer to me for most of the night for reasons only they know — if even they know.

I hailed a homebound cab. Needless to say, I didn't know there would be hell to pay for my inquisitiveness. But apparently, in Beijing, that's what happens when you deal with the Devils.

ERIK NILSSON
(May 16, 2007)

3. Thrill of being a fugitive

They really were on a manhunt.

I hadn't realized the gusto of their pursuit of me until the day my friend Jon called me at work to tell me: "They're really looking for you, man."

But how did Jon find out that the bank was hot on my heels?

"When I went to the bank, they took me to the back room with some security guards and guys in suits. They held up security-camera pictures of you and your girlfriend, and asked me: 'Do you know these foreigners?'"

A nervous Jon said his first response to this interrogation was something to the effect of: "C'mon; just because I'm a foreigner doesn't mean I know every foreigner in Beijing."

His second response was something to the effect of: "Oh, wait. Yeah. I guess I do actually know those two."

China might be a colossal country, but it's a small world after all.

It all started a few weeks before, when my friend Jenny visited Beijing with no more than $50 of American currency and — as she discovered — misplaced hopes of using her credit card here.

So, we had to change her US dollars into yuan, until we could figure out how to get cash from her credit card.

I provided interpretation for the exchange and, at the bank's insistence, my mobile number in case the bank would need to reach us for any reason. After we'd spent three more days at ATMs and in banks searching for one with the alchemic capability to turn Jenny's plastic into banknotes, the bank found a reason to call. And call. And call. And call.

It was Jenny's last day in China when the bank first called claiming they'd given her 1,000 yuan ($132) too many — a contention of which we were more than skeptical — and insisting we come down immediately to settle the matter.

I politely refused, because it was Jenny's last day and I was 20 minutes from picking up my parents, whom I hadn't seen in nine months, from the airport.

I agreed to instead meet with the bank people after my parents returned home. But whichever date I set didn't work out for one reason or another — work commitments, group outings, necessary shopping — and eventually, I wondered why I should give them any more of my precious free time. I mean, they weren't getting any money from me. I certainly never got any from them. I was just an interpreter.

But when I finally told them of my decision, they continued calling to ask when I was coming down. And the more I insisted I wasn't coming, the more they called — morning, noon and night.

This went on for months, until one day, the calls unexpectedly stopped.

Strangely enough, I found I missed the constant hounding to which I'd become accustomed. Perhaps it was the thrill of being a fugitive. I had never felt as much like Harrison Ford than I had during this period of my life.

But at the same time, I still hide my face any time I walk past that bank.

When I lived in the United States, I was always chasing the bank. But sometimes in China, I've found, the bank chases back.

ERIK NILSSON
(July 11, 2007)

4. Slithering out of darkness

It was pitch black.

I mean we couldn't see anything at all. Absolutely nothing. Still, my girlfriend Carol and I were stumbling down an uneven stone stairway in the Mount Qixianling National Forest Reserve, in Hainan province, feeling our way through the inkiness with a bamboo sprig.

The darkness smothered us. And the jungle echoed with the yowls, yelps and caws of its nocturnal beasts as the critters rose from their gentle slumbers to prowl the tropical night.

By this point, we had been descending the slope for about 45 minutes, about 15 minutes of which were spent in total darkness. We had become completely dependent on the bamboo poles we had picked up en route to help us feel our way along the path.

Actually, we had no way of knowing exactly how long we'd been descending the mountainside, because we'd decided against bringing our phones (our only timepieces) so they wouldn't become a liability in the rain forest.

Ironically, that's what got us into this mess. Earlier in the day, we were particularly glad we didn't carry our phones after Carol slipped on a slick stone while crossing a river and plunged in. But as a light source, my phone would have been an invaluable asset.

I was starting to realize that it would take us until sunrise to descend the mountainside at this rate. When we'd scaled Taishan Mountain in May, we had over-packed and lugged huge, overstuffed backpacks crammed with four flashlights up its crags for the five-hour ascent. We thought we'd learned our lesson then. Now, I was even beginning to plot a harebrained torch-making scheme to ensure we didn't have to camp in the rainforest.

But I'm not sure which made the idea more unappealing — the perfect absurdity of the notion or the thought of groping for flammable brush in the dark when trailblazing earlier we'd nearly ambled headlong into the orb web of a green spider larger than Carol's hand.

I had no idea what creepy crawlies were venomous here. But I remembered we had to wear galoshes to slog through the Costa Rican rain forest, and one of my travel mates went home with botfly larvae embedded in her neck.

Suddenly, I remembered my camera. I fumbled it from my bag and pressed the ON button. With the light cast by its screen, we could see the steps — and the wriggling snake crawling up them!

"It's like a nightmare!" I howled. Carol still teases me for that statement.

I jumped back in alarm and readied my bamboo pole for action. In my panic, I worried that if I were to whack this slithering serpent it might fly up towards my face, landing with its fangs clamped to my cheek. It seemed possible — actually, plausible — at the time.

Then, suddenly, out of nowhere, came the floating light of a mobile phone. A man emerged from the darkness, brushed passed the snake and grabbed Carol's hand to lead her down the mountainside.

For the next two hours, we walked with this fellow and a caravan of others who'd also overstayed their welcome at the peak.

We finally arrived at the motorcycle station. We exchanged a round of hoorays and high-fives with our newfound friends, whom we were actually seeing for the first time, before going on our way. Our next mission is Zhangjiajie, and I have no idea what to expect.

But the first things I'm going to pack are my mobile phone and flashlight.

ERIK NILSSON

(Oct 10, 2007)

5. Bumps in the road

I had only two choices — crash or splash.

So into the brook I went, tumbling over our hulky electric bike, off the bridge and down the gully's slope. I splooshed into the waterlogged bed of a roughly 3-m-deep ditch, somehow landing on my feet.

I glanced up at the farmer standing on the bridge with his pushcart, and then down at the bike in the ditch.

It was impossible to tell what damage the two-wheeler's nose had sustained, because it was buried beneath muddy wavelets. I was imagining what its mashed front might look like and wondering how I'd explain this to the woman from whom we'd rented the bike near our hotel in Yangshuo, Guangxi Zhuang autonomous region.

The farmer, whose age had sculpted his crinkled and toothless visage to resemble that of a tortoise, poked his head out like the said animal to peer over the bridge's edge. I stood in the creek, radiating ring-shaped ripples from the middle of my shins as he looked at me, shocked.

He'd also surprised me earlier when he appeared out of nowhere and hobbled onto the bridge, leaving me without any room to circumnavigate his cart.

After hoisting myself out of the steep gully, Dad and I hauled the hefty bike up to discover the only damage was a dangling bumper.

Our family had rented *diandongche* (electric bikes) because we thought we'd be cruising along the paved roads connecting Yangshuo's hinterlands to its downtown. We had no inkling our local guide would be leading us through the slender dirt trails crisscrossing the area's limestone knobs, bamboo thickets and rice paddies.

The problem was that many of these bone-juddering paths were less than half a meter wide, but our bikes were more than half a meter wide.

Only my sister-in-law had been wise enough to opt for a mountain bike, and we discussed how much safer it was as we zipped down a gravel road.

"I'm really glad she got this bike," she said, "because" — BLAM!

At that instant, her front wheel struck a large, sharp rock poking out of the ground, catapulting her off the bicycle. She scuffed her elbow and knee. The bike's back tire deflated and the chain flopped off.

Toward the day's end, we were coasting along the busy main road leading to our hotel.

Someone, for some reason, had scattered hundreds of fake 1-yuan bills all over the road. The bikers in front of my parents slammed on their brakes to inspect the cash, causing another near miss.

When I also stopped to examine the phony banknotes, another biker whizzed past me, howling, in English: "Money! Money! Hahaha!"

The next day we decided to bike again, this time keeping our electric two-wheelers to paved roadways.

But the handbrakes of Mom and Dad's *diandongche* didn't work, and the motor in the bike my wife and I had rented was too wimpy to carry us uphill. While Mom and Dad had to drag their feet to slow their velocity on downhill stretches, my wife and I had to use our feet to push uphill, mimicking the locomotion of a frog.

We eventually figured out our parents' model also had a footbrake, so

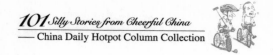

they no longer needed to use the Flintstonian deceleration method. I rode home with them, because my wife and I had traveled too far out on "the little bike that couldn't".

Locals who hadn't thought a thing of seeing two foreigners on a scooter now howled with delight at the sight of three. Two grinners on a motorbike turned their vehicle around for a better look. At the main intersection, they turned to us, jabbed their thumbs into the air and declared, in English: "Yeah! Yeah! Let's go!"

We had hoped for no mishaps when we'd set out to bike Yangshuo's pristine countryside. But we found that sometimes, it's the bumps in the road that make the journey more exciting and memorable.

ERIK NILSSON

(Oct 27, 2009)

6. Touts turn out to be friendly

"Don't carry too much cash with you, and make sure you don't get cheated," a colleague reminded me when I told him I was going to Songshan Mountain in Henan province.

It was a warning I would receive numerous times from others in the newsroom and friends outside before I headed for the province.

The central region seems to carry a reputation for fleecing travelers. That fear, some say, is reflected in the harsh-sounding Henan dialect.

My four-day experience there could not have been farther from those concerns.

Tour and taxi touts who buzz around dazed travelers just outside of the railway station are not confined to the monolithic one in Zhengzhou, Henan's provincial capital. These predators are everywhere in the country, as most domestic and foreign travelers would attest to.

But beyond the ruckus of the railway square, I encountered heartening acts of kindness from the locals. As with most other encounters in China, or many other countries for that matter, once you try to understand what people tell you, the stereotypes fade and the barriers come tumbling down.

When I asked for directions in the pleasant town of Dengfeng, at the foot of Songshan, a bespectacled teenage girl made a detour from her scheduled music class to show me the right bus to take. She even took the time to point out her primary school, an equally agreeable structure nestled among rows of noodle, curio and other mom-and-pop shops.

"That's where I studied," she said.

"Cute, right?"

On the minibus to the famed Shaolin Temple, two chirpy passengers offered their bag of roasted sunflower seeds to me during our friendly 15-minute chat.

"Help yourself," one of them said.

"There's a lot more food where that came from."

A resident monk on a routine climb up the slopes of Wuru Peak, which overlooks the Shaolin Temple grounds, gave me a timely introduction to the area's history and attractions. He also recommended nearby lodging, helping me save money and an extra trip back to Dengfeng.

"You don't look like you need anything too luxurious," he said.

"Just enough for a good night's sleep."

Nature reserve employee Zhao Zixing joined me on part of my trek around Songshan's summit. Seeing that I was traveling on my own, he spoke briefly — in between pants and gasps — about the dangerous stretches of the mountain paths and the choice spots to take in the sights.

"What you want to watch out for are the bees, yeah, apart from the ridiculous songs blaring from the cable car towers. Those bugs can be quite a nuisance," the 55-year-old said.

As I marveled at the view of Henan's central plains from an unopened souvenir stand near the mountain peak, a man in his early 20s shared my bench with his visiting girlfriend. The young man immediately whipped out a cigarette for me as he enjoyed his smoke among the clouds.

I found it too impolite to refuse.

"Great view and great air," he muttered.

Great company, too, I thought.

ALEXIS HOOI

(Sep 17, 2008)

7. Stone phone calls through the ages

When my sister visited China for the first time, I wanted to show her something ancient — something that would allow me to fulfill my self-proclaimed role as Family China Expert.

I needed something ancient — something that seemed strange at first but made perfect sense after my graceful cultural interpretation or at least something that would let me quote Confucius.

So I took her up the icy peaks of Huangshan, Anhui province, where I knew I could launch into my armchair thesis about the famous Yingke Song, Welcoming Guest Pine Tree.

This single pine tree graces teacups and hotel lobbies across the Middle Kingdom because it leans protectively over two stones that look like weary travelers — a perfect embodiment of China's guest culture.

Travelers from all over China still make grueling pilgrimages just to fight crowds for a snapshot with the popular pine, even though the original tree has long since withered and died. They fight and wait in line for a second-string replacement that's the pine tree equivalent of Lassies 2 through 8.

No sooner had I launched into my pontification than I noticed my sister wasn't listening. So I canned my over-eager pedantry and read the sign by the potato-shaped boulder that she was absorbed in. It read: "Shouji Shi,

Mobilephone Stone."

The sign detailed how nature had so graciously endowed the stone with a cell phone body and antennae, thanks to the fact that the rock's different parts eroded at different rates. After we finished reading, my sister brought my ego back down to size: "So what do cell phones represent in traditional Chinese culture, and exactly which poets have verses about the symbolism of antennas and ring tones?"

Modern or ancient aside, the message of Huangshan is clear: In China, a tree is not just a tree. China's trees, stones and rivers take on second lives after building layer upon layer of symbolism as they're extolled by poets, painters

Pang Li

and passing statesmen.

But what's the message behind a stone phone?

In retrospect, Mobilephone Stone shouldn't have been so surprising. Its enjoyment lies in seeing one's own culture embodied in nature. This is why people look at a stone in Jiangxi's Sanqing Mountain and see Zhu Bajie (the famous pig from *Journey to the West*) or "Wife Waiting for Her Husband Stone" in Yunnan's Stone Forest. It's also probably why I see so many pet owners in Beijing dress their dogs in people clothes and why my Chinese dictionary defines animals by their usefulness to humans.

Adoring a pine tree for welcoming guests isn't really so different from heralding rocks that look like cell phones. The difference is that the practice of welcoming guests dates back to Confucius, whereas the practice of sending text messages dates back to, well, me.

Confucius is a central part of one of the world's longest continuous cultures, but that same culture is still absorbing computers and cell phones —— and relevant stones. And Chinese culture will continue to do so, even as I drag my siblings against their will to search for a China without modern trappings. Mobilephone Stone captures exactly this paradox of my life in China: I scour Chinese society for things ancient; Chinese society points to its own modernity.

In the end, Mobilephone Stone crushed my best-laid plan to mentally erase China's modernity. So I decided I needed a change of plan as my sister and I walked wearily down the mountain.

My sister has since returned to the States, but I've promised her I'll send pictures when I find Modem Maple and Laptop Lake.

THOMAS TALHELM
(April 14, 2009)

8. The big smile said it all

My Dad, who passed away six years ago, was one of the most affable people you can imagine. When I was a kid, he used to mortify me by striking up conversations with total strangers everywhere.

Parents' quirks often surface in their children, of course — so eventually, as an adult, I found myself doing the same thing. Just ask my kids: They'll tell you how I constantly embarrass them by chatting with people I've never met before and may never see again — in elevators, in line for movie tickets, at the grocery store.

A freelance photographer, my Dad faced subjects ranging from diplomats and corporate executives to artists, athletes, fishermen and factory workers, so his ability to get along with everybody served him well. At bottom, though, it was not utilitarian purpose that gave rise to his friendliness; it was a profoundly democratic attitude that made him converse as easily with a US senator as with a janitor.

I'd actually been pathologically shy as a child, but once I started work as a newspaper reporter, my inheritance became second nature. After all, much of journalism's raw material comes from listening to strangers. And sometimes the best stories and sources come from serendipitous encounters on the street.

While my days of daily reporting are past, my journalistic habits persist, and I continue to find chance encounters a source of endless fascination.

Now that I'm back in Beijing for a couple of months, however, chatting with strangers takes on new dimensions that I don't always welcome.

On the one hand, if I initiate the interaction, typically with a request for directions, I get gleeful reactions to my Beijing-inflected Mandarin Chinese. On the other hand, Chinese who notice this middle-aged casually dressed woman with dirty-blond hair and green eyes wandering a subway platform or a department store may well seize a chance to practice their English.

Being a sounding board for a language learner is not always my idea of fun. If I'm tired, distracted, or in a bad mood, or if the speaker seems to be talking at me rather than to me and doesn't catch what I say ever-so-slowly in response, I'm seldom inclined to carry on. I prefer two-way communication, for what is a conversation if not an exchange?

An incident last week, however, reminded me that crossing paths with strangers has its own rewards.

I was waiting to board the light rail when a fellow with shaggy graying hair wheeled by on one of those folding mini-bikes. "American?" he asked in English. When I said yes, he gave me a big gap-toothed smile and pedaled on.

Half an hour later, he passed me on his bike in the street; evidently we'd disembarked at the same station. He halted to give me a hearty greeting before cycling on.

In another 15 minutes, as I was walking on a college campus, there he was again, rounding a corner. He told me he was visiting an uncle who worked there. Again, he cycled off.

On each occasion, I got another smile. I didn't feel like a lesson plan.

I felt like we were old friends.

JUDY POLUMBAUM
(March 29, 2007)

9. Porn dated at explicit exhibition

Traversing China, I continue to be delighted and surprised with its amazing juxtapositions of the very old and new. My recent trip to Tongli, another of China's beautiful water towns in Jiangsu province, is no exception.

The slow boat rides down ancient canals, past exquisite mansions, cobbled streets and arching bridges. Many of the lovely old buildings are still in use, including the China Sex Museum. The sex museum? Yup, Tongli has it all, including one of the world's few museums dedicated solely to all matters sexual.

If your purpose is to pay 20 yuan and romp around in a titillating porno palace, you will be terribly disappointed. The purpose of the museum's founder, professor Liu Dalin, is to add to our body of knowledge, not necessarily our knowledge of bodies. He is an esteemed professor of sociology and the author of many books on love, marriage and sex.

There's lot to see. The museum is divided into sections, including Sex in Primitive Society, Marriage and Women, Sex in Daily Life and Unusual Sexual Behavior.

Then there's the matter of taste. In English we talk about "good taste" and "bad taste", which are highly subjective. Visiting people's homes and seeing what people wear shows that what is elegant to one is hopelessly garish to another. How can one design a sex museum that is in good taste and not just an exhibition for the prurient?

Visit the China Sex Museum, and I'm sure you'll agree they pulled it off. The exhibitions are housed in a gorgeous group of Qing Dynasty (1644-1911) buildings, formerly the Lize Girl's School, and surrounded by a lovely garden.

The statuary in the garden all relate in some way to matters sexual. Some are sweet goddesses and fully clothed courtesans, while others are startling in their graphic portrayals. The garden sets the tone. It says that this is a place of beauty and respect for that oldest of human endeavors, but be prepared for explicitness. Fair enough.

Entering the first building, the exhibits relating to primitive society are often carvings of both people and animals of all kinds having sex. Lest you get the giggles, it carefully explains that these were objects of worship because the ancients worshipped sex — and nothing much has changed over the intervening period.

Pang Li

The section called Marriage and Women might make a feminist cringe. It appears from the exhibition that most of the sexual history of women is about their sublimation and degradation. The museum points this out and seems to have scholarly sympathy for their plight through the ages.

Moving on to Sex in Daily Life, one finds the sex instruction scrolls called *Pillow Books in the West*. These make present-day texts to educate the youngsters seem like very pale pudding, indeed. They are explicit and move well beyond the "missionary position". Many of them are wildly funny.

Now that we have been inured to multiple portrayals of "the act", we move into Part 4, Unusual Sexual Behavior, which is described as "opposite to the common sexual behavior of most people". This seems to be rapidly changing, as any glance at modern mores shows that "most people" are quickly expanding the definition of "common", and of "unusual", for that matter.

We all know that China is where gunpowder, paper, moveable-type printing and the compass were invented. To add to this list of pride is the invention of the chastity belt and "sex tools", some of which were carved from precious jade.

Today's news abounds with stories about how to protect youth from seeing sexual content. With the museum's 9,000 years of evidence of interest in the topic, I say, "Good luck."

SANDRA LEE
(Aug 11, 2009)

10. Age no bar at Chinese clubs

Men and women, dressed in the latest fashions, swinging their hips, pumping their arms, shuffling their feet, trying to impress one another — usually, this image is accompanied by sounds of the Billboard Top 40 or the latest techno thumping from the speakers.

But I was curious: Was this merely a Western picture of nightclubbing? Was it different in China?

I needed to go out on the biggest club night of the week, Saturday, to find the answer. My anticipation built up over the course of the day, as I half expected the club to be similar to those in the United States and half hoped for something drastically different.

After paying the cover, I entered the party, where I was greeted with techno blaring so loudly from the speakers that you had to yell in someone's ear to communicate. This was like American clubs.

I meandered down toward the mass of people moving to the music. But at the first step, my leg wobbled, and I quickly put down my second foot to stabilize myself. Never before had I seen a surface like this: The floor was supported by a series of hydraulics, which bumped to the bass of the music.

It was like walking on ice. You are unsure and slip around before you get used to it and take smaller steps to gain balance. My Chinese friends laughed at me. They knew what to expect.

Soon, the headlining DJ, Gareth Emery, began spinning his set. Pushing our way to the center of the dance floor, I found the place packed with expat kids between 14 and 18, wearing Yankee's hats, polos or "I love NY" shirts, dancing in large circles.

Scattered in between were Chinese in their 20s. Outnumbering these were older Chinese men who stood around the edges of the dance floor and on the balcony with tables.

The No 1 rule of China's club scene: Age no bar.

Throughout the establishment, Asian mullets frosted with red or blond tips were spotted next to blond and brown mops of hair worn by expat kids. The older Chinese were either balding or outfitted with neat and trim cuts.

Almost no one seemed to be a good dancer, including myself. But the worst dancers, by far, were the old men who bopped up and down only bending their knees. Never before had I seen faces of those who had just hit puberty next to men whose faces looked like the pleats on the young people's khakis.

Hot and sweaty, I stepped outside for air. Before I got a chance to reflect on my first night out in Beijing, a group of expat teens approached me and began trash talking.

I laughed at their feeble attempts to insult me. I threw a couple of words back their way but became paralyzed with laughter.

They did not know how to handle my laughing or the fact that I continued to sit through all of this, so they shouted: "There're eight of us, and one of you." This only made me laugh harder. I am by no means a tough person, but these kids were even less threatening.

As the talking neared the point of put up or shut up, my big Chinese friend came over, thinking that I was meeting new people. The preppy teenagers quickly backed off. We sat down laughing at the fake tough guys,

and then went back in the club.

Clubbing in China was unique, as with many things here in Beijing, I have accepted the experience as different and am grateful for it.

RAFFI WILLIAMS

(Sep 15, 2009)

11. It's all downhill from here

Since I discovered sea cucumbers are definitely not vegetables, I pledged to do away with my preconceptions about anything in China, even if dealing with something I believed was already familiar to me.

Foolishly, I forgot this as I sat on the coach this weekend, bound for Lianhuashan ski resort north of Beijing. I indulged myself with memories of long days in the Alps, maneuvering over moguls, gliding over glaciers and skiing down endless and varied runs.

The day's program showed we were to hit the slopes at 11 am, stop for a Chinese banquet at 12:30 and then be off the mountain by 4 in order to hand in our kits by 4:30.

A banquet? In the midst of a day of skiing? My friend and I balked.

Lunch on European slopes was a quick sandwich grabbed between trying to cover all the routes.

When we arrived, we could make out one large slope and perhaps five short runs. "I expect there'll be more round the other side," I said.

In the kit room, an army of workers distributed everything we'd need, from skis to clothing.

Luckily, we were not in St Moritz, and this was no fashion parade. I donned my sickly pale blue jacket, elbows threadbare from decades of wear, over newer but no less nauseating, iridescent lime green salopettes. I felt like an '80s jumble of disco ball and shell suit.

Prepared, we rushed to the chair lift, which was to take us up to the main slope. The lift operator refused to let us on because we hadn't practiced on the preliminary slopes, which were packed. After some persuasion, we piled on.

Within half an hour, I knew the contours of the one slope and was getting used to the sight of the shepherd and his sheep in the field adjacent to the run, below the lift.

Li Min

By 12:30, I was cold and bored, and welcomed the idea of a sit-down meal. The food was abundant and we munched on juicy prawns, stir-fried vegetables and beef, washed down with Tsingtao beer.

I'd been watching the hordes on the smaller slopes and concluded I must be missing out on something. Other people hadn't rushed to the biggest slope after a few goes on the small runs as I'd expected.

I stopped pretending I might be in the Alps and decided to muck in with the crowds. I nudged my way into the throng waiting for the lift on one of the smaller slopes, ski poles braced lest anyone dare try to get in front of me.

I grabbed my lift, and swayed and teetered to the top. I was nearly taken out by the schemers who stood right next to the lift's path, looking to grab any spare seat that someone at the bottom had been too slow to catch. I grunted and stuck out my poles.

From the top, it was another gauntlet to descend. Ski classes, mid-slope picnickers and unpredictable children were all obstacles to negotiate.

I enjoyed the experience so much that I tried another two easy runs before returning, with a new philosophy, to the big slope.

On the way up, I photographed the shepherd. I stood at the top, watching the ant-like skiers below. I decided that skiing in China is as much about the journey as the destination, so I launched myself down and focused on weaving a smooth wave down the slope, rather than speed.

At the end of the afternoon, I didn't hit the bar for schnapps to quell my adrenalin rush after bombing down every slope at 160 kph as I would have in Europe. But I did feel happy and refreshed after a fun and novel day out.

And I reaffirmed my pledge to do away with those unhelpful blinkers — preconceptions.

RACHEL O'NEILL
(Feb 4, 2010)

12. **Reality check on a dream journey**

Travel, I have found, is not everyone's cup of tea.

For every person who dreams of the open road, there is someone who dreams that scientists will finally get their act together and invent those teleportation machines everyone uses in *Star Trek*.

These people are usually the ones visibly seething on public buses, even on short journeys, when merely nudging them as you pass through the doors (where they always seem to insist on standing) can result in a tirade of insults and accusations about your inconsiderate nature.

I'm definitely all for the open road. I like using public transport even at peak times. And I especially enjoy long bus and train journeys that offer travelers the chance to reflect, to consider their lives while the rich and often-unique scenery flashes by.

When I arrived in China, I fell in love with overnight bus and rail travel. The bottom bunks of the cozy sleeper compartments are filled with chatting Chinese, while the smells of dried fish and instant noodles fill the air, almost totally covering the odor of stinky feet.

But the main reason I love long journeys over ground is because, in my experience, they usually feature strange events.

Such as the time I woke up on the bottom bunk of a bus from Yangshuo to Guangzhou and it was snowing inside the vehicle. Yes, snowing.

Well, that's what I thought until I looked up and realized the guy on the top bunk was pumicing his feet. He was giving extra attention to between his toes, I noticed. I was just thankful that in my dozy stupor I was not tempted to try and catch one of the "snowflakes" on my tongue.

Pang Li

On the plus side, I am also a heavy sleeper, which makes overnight rail and train journeys a cinch for me. However, I didn't know just how heavy a sleeper I was until after that same bus journey.

While chatting with Mike and Carol, a lovely Irish couple who, seeing I was traveling alone, offered to share a taxi to downtown Guangzhou, the conversation went a little like this:

Mike: "Well that was an experience we'll never forget."

Me: "You mean the bus ride? Was it your first time on a Chinese sleeper bus?"

Mike: "Yeah, and our last, I hope."

Me: "It wasn't so bad. It was better than the time I was on a mini-bus in Laos and one of the back wheels fell off and overtook us on the road. It took us an hour to find the wheel in the bushes as they didn't have a spare. At least this trip was uneventful."

Mike, looking at me: "Do you not remember the crash last night, then? The bus was clipped by a lorry, and the bus actually spun in the middle of the road. We were all terrified, screaming. It was like something from a disaster movie. The driver spent more than two hours rowing with the lorry driver, while the engineer fixed the bodywork so we could carry on. Then everyone shook hands, got back in their respective vehicles and drove away."

Carol explained I had happily slept through the entire episode, even waking up with a cheery yawn as we approached our destination.

It kind of explained why many people were crying when I woke up and the fact there was a big dent in the side of the bus.

CRAIG MCINTOSH

(Jan 26, 2010)

13. Beihai and I come of age

A thousand years of history didn't matter to a 2-year-old, especially one with an overactive bladder.

There is a photo of me as a toddler in Beihai Park, arguably one of the oldest and best-preserved imperial gardens in the country, with a suspicious puddle next to my feet.

Going back even further in time, there is a picture of my mother holding me under one of the weeping willows that swooned toward the edge of the lake.

Beihai Park may have been built for emperors, but it was my playground. Seeing the colossal white tower in the middle of the lake was as much of a daily routine as eating and napping. While other children were hauled off to preschool on the backs of their parents' bicycles, my grandfather gave me piggyback rides to the park's west gate and taught me my first English words — "hello" and "thank you".

When I was 4, I joined my parents in the US, where a park meant any patch of green with a bench on it. I looked forward to summer visits to Beijing. It meant frequent trips to the "real" park, where my cousin and I got blisters on our palms from scaling the metal play structures. My grandmother would buy us snacks — bouquets of lotus bulbs fresh from the lake. Pried from their spongy bed, the jewel-green seeds squeaked between our teeth.

As I got older, Beihai and I both went through our awkward phases. Wenjin Street roared with traffic, and the lake suffered from too many visitors and too little care. Near the Five Dragon Pavilions, the water swirled with candy wrappers, bottles and beer cans. People paddling in the swan-shaped boats had to skirt clumps of neon green and blue algae.

That was 10 years ago. Since then, I have visited the park less and less often, opting for air-conditioned strolls through department stores instead. But recently, my grandmother, now nearly 80 years old, convinced me to take a morning walk there with her.

Stepping in through the south gate, I noticed a large flower display, including a bush pruned into the shape of a dragon that heralded the Olympics. I glanced down at the water. This time, there was no polluted mess — just green waves, lapping quietly at cool white marble.

Beihai has become a place that Beijingers are proud to show off to the world. The white Buddhist tower now appears on one of the commemorative coins for the Olympic Games. Even I, who barely still qualify as a Beijinger, am eager to share this trove of Chinese history and personal memories.

Although it is a bit of a trek to the heart of the city, I want to show my friends the water lilies blooming thickly beneath the bridges. I want them to see the elderly folks at their quirky exercises — walking backwards, dancing and hamming it up for foreigners' cameras. Who knows? They might like eating squeaky lotus seeds.

And the park has nice restrooms. They probably won't see any kids peeing in the bushes.

XIONG ZHI

(Aug 14, 2008)

2. FUNNY BUSINESS

14. Peddlers pack a punch

Suddenly, this strange little lady started slapping me around.

And the harder I bargained, the harder this vicious vendor whacked me.

It was all in good fun, and part of the theatrics of the haggling game at this open-air market behind Beijing's Wangfujing shopping street. But despite being about one-third my size and weight, this peddler packed a mighty punch.

I had taken my visiting family and friends on a shopping mission. For my culture-shocked guests, China's markets seemed to be truly bizarre bazaars, and they had some trouble getting used to flexible pricing.

But they soon found that a trip to a Chinese open-air market is like playing *Let's Make a Deal* and *The Price is Right* simultaneously. And sometimes, it can even be a bit like Nintendo's *Mike Tyson's Punch Out!!*, too.

This spirited saleswoman was selling scrolls — preferably, to fresh-off-the-boat Westerners, such as my visiting friends Jenny and Andrew.

She had just about talked them into paying several hundred times the value of these artworks, when I showed up and started driving a harder bargain.

Her: "How much you give me?"

Me: "20."

Her: "Gasp! Gasp! Oh, my God! No!" (As if her stomach had burst.)

Me: "How much, then?"

Her: "300 yuan."

Me: "Gasp! Gasp! Oh, my God! No!" (As if my stomach had burst.)

Her: "No, really, 300. Good price!"

Me: "No, 20 is a good price. I know. I'm not a tourist. They're offering 30 over there."

Then, this sadistic saleswoman started clobbering me. After a half hour taking blows from these fists of fury and having only knocked off 50 yuan, I decided to seek better deals elsewhere — or at least refuge.

The next week, I came back with my parents to finagle with my friends behind Wangfujing.

And one by one, my unwary family members wandered into the boxer's stall ready to splash too much cash, and I would come to the rescue. I just hoped to give them a fighting chance. The vendor just hoped for a chance to fight.

Every time that I'd offer a somewhat lower-than-reasonable price, she'd hit the ceiling — then she'd start hitting me.

It was very entertaining to my visitors to watch this sprightly saleswoman throttling this oafish foreign galoot. But I would not be beaten into submission or overpay for the scrolls.

And once all of my guests had independently stumbled into the stall of Beijing's boxing businesswoman and we had no more shopping to do there, the vendor began suddenly appearing wherever else I was in the market. She'd deliver a few good cuffs then disappear back into the crowd.

The whole thing was particularly amusing to the mostly Chinese crowd, especially when she borrowed another vendor's calligraphy brush to take my corporal punishment up a few notches.

By the end of our third trip to the market, I left with an armful of traditional trinkets and sore spots.

But kneading my freshly tenderized shoulders while walking toward a cab, I reflected on this shopping experience that proved to be more than I'd bargained for. And I realized: That's the price you sometimes pay in Beijing's bazaars.

ERIK NILSSON
(April 25, 2007)

15. Priceless joys of bargaining

For 100 *kuai*, I'll tell you the secret to bargaining in China.

What's that you say? Fifteen yuan? (Gasp!)

No kidding prices, please. Serious prices, 100 *kuai* — friend, for you, that's already a discount. I usually charge 200!

But you're a good friend, so I'll give you the cheaper price.

C'mon, see, this secret's really high quality.

Everybody has developed their own routine for cleaving a meaty percentage off the prices offered by vendors. Most spells are an almost algebraic formula, in which dramatic theatrics, humor and smiles are added, subtracted and multiplied to equal the right price. Some people have labored especially hard to hone their strategies to ensure they have the trickiest bag of tricks possible.

My pal Zhou, for example, told me that if she's buying something, such as a pair of pants, after the seller makes the first offer, she'll scoff and claim her mother ran a garment factory. This, she says, usually slashes the price dramatically in one fell swoop.

The trick, she says, is to remain hyperactively confident in the bluff — if not, clever vendors will easily see right through the act.

When my buddy Pat found out a large number of the Silk Market vendors hail from Anhui province, he took it upon himself to learn a few bargaining-related phrases in their local dialect.

When these roll off his tongue, it raises eyebrows and lowers prices.

Sunnia was raised in a Cantonese-speaking household in California and lived in Hong Kong for several years, so she keeps an ear out for the dialect in the din of marketplaces.

When a Cantonese blip appears on her linguistic radar, she locks her sites on the target and lets loose with rapid-fire *guangdonghua*, leaving them none the wiser as to her eligibility for the "foreigner tax".

If there's no Cantonese conversation floating through the air, she approaches any seller and just says she's from South China, which excuses her from any slip-ups in Mandarin and usually results in the same tax exemption.

When Pat and Sunnia team up to bargain, they also use the "ice cream" method.

Upon being given an inflated price, they insist that if the item's that expensive, it must come with free ice cream.

This gets everybody smiling and laughing, and "gets them on our side", as Pat says. Such warm exchanges melt most retailers' resolve, but the two have yet to have anyone actually give them a frozen treat.

Yes, there's an arsenal of tactics people can use when battling for the best value.

But the secret to bargaining is that strategy isn't as important as attitude. The main thing here is to realize you're not just shopping for yourself.

Some foreign friends with pockets thickly lined by handsome expat packages say they don't mind paying a little more for purchases, because it will beef up vendors' incomes. I used to believe that instead, you should fight to save every last fen, because that means you're on a level playing field. Nobody's being condescendingly gracious about their elevated wealth, and there's no perception that anyone's being taken.

But when I chatted about this with a Chinese friend, he explained to me that by giving in and settling on too high a price, you're actually ripping the vendor off.

The way he put it, the work of a hawker can be pretty boring, and banter with customers, the theatrics and humor is the only thing that keeps it interesting.

And enjoying what one does for a living — that's something it's impossible to put a price on.

ERIK NILSSON
(Dec 4, 2008)

16. Cost in translation

I walked my numb feet down the Great Wall, which the cold had left so deserted I hardly recognized it.

Unlike all the sane people who stayed home, I had decided to brave the winter wind strong enough to knock me over, just so I could take my sister to see the world's greatest wall.

As we approached a watchtower, we saw something we hadn't seen so far on the Wall — a vendor.

She stood next to the watchtower, bundled in a large red coat and scarf, selling small gold-colored Great Walls to anyone walking past. When we came within earshot, the woman set into her sales pitch: "*Liang kuai, liang kuai!* Five! Five!"

Being a white-faced foreigner in China, I reap undue benefits galore. I get guest-of-honor status in small town restaurants, where I've had to argue with locals who insist on paying my bill. I get frequent and hearty "halloos" when I walk on most streets. And I'm lavished with effusive praise for my Chinese skills before I can even get past "*ni hao*".

But of all the benefits, my favorite is preferential pricing for foreigners.

Preferential pricing, like prejudice, is often hard to prove. But the gall of this Great Wall vendor was so obvious, it made me laugh. In the same shout, she had declared that the Chinese price was *liang kuai*, 2 yuan ($0.29), and the

English-speaking price was 5 yuan — more than double the local price.

When my cousin — who speaks excellent Chinese — asked her about the obvious discrepancy, the woman came up with an excuse, saying she was referring to different sizes of the trinkets. This was despite the fact that there was only one size in her cardboard box.

In China, foreign guests have the honor of paying all sorts of special fees because of the color of their passports. When I took a local bus to a remote Yunnan hiking trail popular with foreigners, the bus stopped right before an iron bridge stretched across a stunning canyon. A young man in an unlabeled

Li Min

uniform trotted out from a one-room office next to the bridge and stepped onto the bus. He scanned the passengers and marched directly to my seat.

"You must pay the bridge fee. 100 yuan."

I protested, but the man would not budge. I paid so that the bus would not be kept hostage.

Foreigners get this honor in countries besides China. I saw one unabashed sign in Laos at the entrance to a waterfall that read entirely in English: "Foreigner price: 5,000 kip ($0.59). Local people: 3,000 kip."

I'm told that some countries' airlines even charge foreigners more for the same tickets. But if you can't jet around the world, don't despair. The practice of overcharging outsiders is so universal you don't need to travel to the other side of the world to experience it.

I've fallen prey to the foreigner price fix without leaving my home country.

My sister and I bought some famous South Carolina boiled peanuts at a roadside stand, where we had the honor of paying the northern-accent tax. At least, that's the only explanation we could come up with for why we paid twice as much as the southern customer in front of us.

So, it was hard to be too upset with the stubborn vendor on the Great Wall when she so nonchalantly tried to gouge us. At the very least, she was embarrassed enough to come up with an excuse for her trick. That's at least a step up from the unashamed sign in Laos that went out of its way to explain to English-speakers that we were being ripped off.

And for most foreign vacationers, paying an extra 3 yuan would mean far less than it would to the vendor. I, for one, would be willing to pay an extra 3 yuan for the laugh that woman's chutzpah gave me.

THOMAS TALHELM

(Feb 3, 2010)

17. Making deals and friends

Recently, we went shopping near the Forbidden City and bought some silk for a gorgeous kimono-style robe before moving on to search for artwork.

On a little street located on the east side of the Imperial Palace, we found a small shop that had some appealing things.

Our new Chinese friend, whom I call "Pebble", explained to the shop girl that I was looking for something unique and different. The shop girl made a call, and soon a man came to show us a selection of scrolls and paintings. I romantically fantasized that he lived in a little house nearby, but more likely he had just come from one of the thriving corner bars, with signs that read, "Beer is GOOD here!"

After showing me several items, he stopped and looked at me, and thought. Then he pulled out a long, dusty scroll from underneath a workbench. As he opened it, I watched as the beautiful watercolor strokes of horse bodies begin to appear, then Chinese women mounted on the horses.

The colors were lovely, and it was just what I wanted. He said it was an old work of his, from the 1960s, before he even had a shop.

Then the haggling began.

Haggling is a way of life in China. I think that to understand haggling is to gain a cultural insight into the persistence and perseverance of the

Chinese people. They enjoy this. It almost seems to have a necessary social significance.

A Westerner soon comes to understand that the sweetest accolade they can receive is the phrase, "I no make any money here, lady!" Anyway, I chose another less exotic screen as a gift, and the price actually dropped, then dropped again, as Pebble made another plea for *"pianyi yidianr"* (a little cheaper), please. At last, the bargain was struck. A sense of accomplishment and celebration ensued for all.

In the interaction, we had become connected somehow. The man is a noted calligrapher, and later in the visit he offered to make a scroll as a gift. He studied his visitors carefully, then pulled out some beautiful scroll frames and assembled the tools of his trade.

He proceeded to question Pebble about her father and then asked about me. In the rapid-fire interchange in Chinese, I found only the occasional word intelligible, but he seemed satisfied, and after a muttered *"haode, haode"* (good), he bent to his bench and lifted his brush.

He paused and then began to write beautiful Chinese characters in black ink on the creamy off-white paper. He added his signature, then a red seal — then another to show his authentication of the scroll. Beautiful.

But next he told Pebble to tell me that he had written about a cycle of good, and how the good within each of us can be shared with those around us so that it continues to come back. He gave me a beautiful split-toothed smile and stuck out his hand to shake mine. As I write this, I am still moved by the experience.

There are so many wonderful things to see here in China. I am so thankful that I have been here long enough to see all of the sights and to be able to feel a sense of who these people are and to see them. It is just an amazing journey.

JANE HANSON
(July 23, 2008)

18. Where you shop 'til you drop

Hong Kong is a shoppers' heaven, especially after Christmas. Although I'm not a shopaholic, I couldn't resist the temptation of the big sales and decided to treat myself.

My husband and I arrived in the city on New Year's Eve. While we were waiting at the hotel's reception to check in, we realized we had just missed the first buying spree. Nearby was a long line of people carrying various stuffed suitcases — some so big they defy description.

Accordingly, we immediately made up our minds that the first thing we needed was an enormous bag, large enough to fit an elephant inside.

Strolling through downtown Hong Kong was more like wandering around Wangfujing Street in Beijing. My ears picked up various Chinese dialects, including Shanghai's, Hangzhou's and Shandong's.

The jewelry business was booming. Most jewelers we visited were packed with mainland customers, many of them with their noses glued to the display glass, especially at the diamond counters. I had a real problem even getting a peep of what was on offer, as nobody wanted to make room for me. Some even gave me an odd look, as if I was intruding on their turf.

So, we gave up the idea of buying rings. Our next stop was Harbor City, one of the most famous shopping malls in Hong Kong.

It was a sea of faces, not a harbor at all. The sight of people happily spending would have cheered any investment banker with a stake in the city's fortunes.

I felt sorry for all those men waiting anxiously outside shops, surrounded by mountains of bags. Their eyes tried hard to trace their partners who had already disappeared into the sea of people.

"You need a life preserver before you jump into the shop," my husband joked.

Shopping with these enthusiastic customers was such an eye-opening experience.

In one sportswear shop, a woman in her 50s carried a huge Louis Vuitton handbag, pointed at several pairs of trainers the moment she spotted them and yelled: "I want this, that and that. Wrap them for me please."

I was so relieved she didn't point at the poor shop assistant.

"They are not shopping. It's more like robbing," a man next to me sighed.

Influenced by the shopaholics, we both agreed we should buy something or we'd feel guilty.

From then on, and until the day came to pack our luggage, we shopped as if in a trance. I had no idea why I'd bought two bags, three pairs of shoes and four makeup sets. I certainly didn't need them all.

On my flight back to Beijing, I could barely sleep for fear of having a heart attack caused by the bills I had piled up.

Before we landed, the girl next to me called the airhostess over.

"I have read the duty-free book. I would like to buy some perfume," she said, cheerfully.

My husband was right — some visitors to Hong Kong feel compelled to shop until the very last minute.

Suddenly, I didn't feel so bad after all.

XIE FANG

(Jan 20, 2009)

19. When money-hungry restaurateurs smell prey

You might not lose your way in a city if you have a map in hand. But you might get lost in a crowd of waiters sent from different restaurants to tout for business.

This is something I cannot understand. Chinese are usually slightly shy and conservative. But the waiters appear too warm and even aggressive when soliciting diners.

Instead of standing next to the door to greet guests, the waiters usually step out and cry out. If a diner looks puzzled about where to eat, it will just be the beginning of a "war".

My friends once took me out for lunch in Maojiapu, a hot spot at the foot of the Dragon Well Mountain in Zhejiang province's Hangzhou. Teahouses line the roadsides, serving not only tea but also delicious food.

As we slowed down the car, trying to find a place to park, a flock of middle-aged waitresses spotted us. They were so excited and started to chase our car, some even clapped the windows to call our attention, which made me feel as if I were a film star. I was quite flattered.

"They are not thrilled by you. They are thrilled by the money in your pocket," my friend warned.

We got out and stepped into a crowd of nonstop talking women. I felt sorry for myself as I could close my eyes but not my ears.

Each of them strongly recommended their own teahouse and tried to drag us into different directions.

To end the embarrassment, we quickly decided to follow the one who looked the kindest and most sincere among these superwomen.

Later, when we found the food was not as pleasant as the woman had guaranteed, we looked for her to complain. Unfortunately, she was busy chasing other new arrivals.

In Beijing, the job of greeting diners has apparently been taken over by men, especially on Guijie, a famous dining street in Dongcheng district. There are always young waiters in different uniforms standing anxiously on the roadside, like a school of fish hungry for food.

I was told that in the past, some waiters even carried young women customers into their restaurants in order to compete with others.

I don't think it will happen to me, because I am too big for the waiter's shoulders. But I'll never dare to challenge it.

So, every time I visit there, I just go straight to the restaurant I have booked. Once, I finished dinner with my friends and thinking naïvely that no one could bother us any more, we took a walk along the street. However, we were still followed by persistent waiters.

"I have eaten already!" I cried out, impatiently.

"Our food is so good that people can hardly resist it," a tall man said, smiling.

Then he lowered his voice, saying: "How about a second dinner? I promise I'll never tell your weight-conscious friends!"

XIE FANG

(Aug 2, 2007)

20. Fishing for the real deal

Even though people joke that the antiques in Panjiayuan are 200 percent fake, the market attracts thousands of visitors who try their luck. That includes me.

The biggest antiques market in Beijing, located on the southeastern 3rd Ring Road, opens early on weekend mornings. Insiders believe the earlier you get there, the better are your chances of finding something real. Accordingly, I arrived at 7 am on a Saturday.

The market had already become an ocean of faces. Hundreds of stands were lined up in a huge shed. Small booths occupied the entrance and the alley behind the antique shops.

Wandering among them was tough, as every booth had a dazzling range of so-called antiques. Just as I was about to lose interest, a penholder attracted my attention.

Covered in a thick layer of dust, the palm-sized container had delicate carvings of an old man fishing under a pine tree.

The design was ingenious because not only could the container, which resembled a miniature tree trunk, hold brushes but also the bamboo fish hamper carved on its face had a little hole to hold your pens.

I liked it at first sight. When I asked the vendor where it came from and what it was made of, he said he didn't know as he had just picked it up in the countryside.

"But it must be made of good wood because it is so heavy," he added.

I instantly felt a surge of wild joy. The vendor didn't realize, I surmised, what a great piece that was. If made in the early Qing Dynasty (1644-1911), its market value should be far more than what I had earned in all my years as a writer. How lucky I was!

I tried hard to hide my excitement. The vendor asked for 400 yuan ($57). I bid 50 yuan ($7), which I thought was low enough to give him a heart attack.

He turned his head away and let me go. I did walk away but kept telling myself not to turn until he called me back. Finally, I got it for 80 yuan ($11).

Later, I walked into an antique shop to buy some walnut oil used to protect wooden furniture.

While talking to the manager, I could not help telling him the story of my prize catch and showed it off.

After inspecting my treasure for a while, the middle-aged man was obviously sorry to tell me some heartbreaking news: It was made of plastic, not wood.

"Just scratch it, and you will see plastic inside," he explained. "Don't be upset. It should be a good piece if you clean it."

Back home, cleaning the fake antique turned out to be another disaster. The brush pot was actually painted with black ink to make it look old. And the bottom, which looked like wood, was painted in yellow.

My sink was stained with dirty water with such a nasty smell that I felt like throwing the penholder out of my window.

Ironically, a few weeks later, I saw exactly the same piece again in Panjiayuan.

My friends are right. They always tell me to buy less and observe more.

But it was the plastic fisherman who taught me a lesson I'll never forget.

XIE FANG
(Oct 16, 2008)

3. ON THE ROAD

21. Murphy's Law drives me crazy

A 100-question knowledge test is the foreigner's gateway to a Chinese driver's license, but the all-important paperwork needs to be in order.

For impatient "need-it-now" novices, this paper trail can lead to many dead-ends. If you want a ticket to ride in the Middle Kingdom, heed the words of someone who has been there and failed that.

I always live by Murphy's Law. If something can go wrong, it will. The glass is not half full, nor half empty; it's poisoned. This attitude makes living in China a sheer delight, because most things go unexpectedly right. When they don't, I am ready for it.

My driving ambition, however, had Murphy stamped all over it.

The checklist includes: passport, residence permit, original driver's license, medical certificate, and five photographs. Get the photos first. I went to the hospital for my medical certificate first, only to be sent away to get the photos.

The 2.5 cm x 2.5 cm happy snaps must have white backgrounds. I chose blue, because it was my favorite color, but this was a time-wasting mistake. Also take note of photo size. This is not passport size; it is smaller. Got this wrong, too.

Take one picture to a hospital or doctor for the medical certificate. The eye chart features the capital Es in different sizes and positions on different lines. The color vision test involves distinguishing between green and red within mosaic patterns.

The next step is the foreign office of the branch of the traffic administration department of public security. At the counter, a traffic police officer asks me to write my token Chinese name in Chinese.

I had never done this before and struggled, but wrote Bai Li Cheng (White-ley honestly).

I book my test and have two weeks to study the road rules. The rules book cannot be purchased at this office. The only place in Beijing to buy the exam reference manual in English is the FESCO office, in the Beijing CBD.

I take a 50-yuan ($6.4) taxi ride and buy the 150-yuan ($19) book.

It has 1,000 questions about laws, signs, highway driving, penalties, accident procedures, license details, safety, first aid and guidelines for "civil" behavior. I have to understand Chinese road sign characters for goodness sake, and I can't even write my name.

Then there are questions like this: When other drivers correct you, you should:

(a) learn modestly and accept the opinion seriously;

(b) not listen, and

(c) accept but not try to improve.

On Australian roads, a driver's correction sounds like this. Get the blank out of the blank blank way you blank, blank, blank. The answer is (b).

Next. For an open abdominal wound, such as protrusion of the small intestine tube, we should:

(a) put it back;

(b) no treatment,

(c) not put it back, but cover it with a bowl or jar, and bind it with a cloth belt.

Who do they think I am? A stomach surgeon? Must be (b).

I sit the computer test with 50 other "foreigners", who are mostly Chinese with foreign passports. It's a 45-minute test and one guy finishes in a quarter of an hour. He passes because a little smiley face pops up on screen if an examinee is successful.

A sad face pops up on my screen. I score 88, two questions short of a pass mark. I'm absolutely delighted. I know exactly which two questions I need to revisit.

PATRICK WHITELEY

(Jan 4, 2007)

22. What the beep are you saying?

My Chinese language teacher tells me there are four tones in Mandarin, but I reckon I've discovered a fifth — the sweet tone of the beeping car horn. You don't need lessons for this tone, just a trigger-happy hand and a need to share the love.

It is a relatively new tone in China, however, it is by far the most commonly used tone by millions of new motorists on the move. Within this fifth tone, there are many variations, depending on the circumstances.

There is the light rising beep tone, which acts as a courtesy reminder to the driver ahead. It says: "Hey there buddy, hope you are having a good day. Don't mind me, I'm just passing by on your left and will soon be on my way." They can hear it, but it does not linger and causes no major reaction.

Then there is the mid-level honk tone, which does linger but only for 2 seconds. It's often used on multiple-lane roads when you're about to pass a guy but he decides to cross over in the passing lane, too. He will never use his indicator signal or mirrors. Why use mirrors, when the fifth tone works just fine?

This firm but friendly honk kind of says: "Whoa there my good man, you'll probably want to stay in your right lane because it could get messy." Remember, firm but fair.

You don't want to push the horn for too long because you don't know the driver's state of mind. His girlfriend may have insisted on watching Zhang Yimou's *Curse of the Golden Flower,* and he could be suicidal.

The final toot tone used in the Chinese language is the long, sustained howler, which seems to go on forever. If you don't keep it resonating for at least 8 seconds, you're not doing it right. It is used when everything is hopeless, and by some magic, fixes everything.

I saw it used one morning during rush hour when a narrow street was blocked by a convoy of three cars exiting an apartment block. There was no space, however, the three honk-eteers managed to push their way in and then let it rip. Their sound was triumphant. The lights at the nearby intersection turned green, the traffic jam dispersed, and everybody behind the wheel inched their way to work.

Language experts say it takes 2,200 hours to really speak fluent Chinese — that's 40 hours a week for 13 months — however, it may take a lifetime to fully understand the mystical power of this fifth tone.

One of the niceties of the fifth tone is the controlled and measured way in which it is used. In most car-centric cities in the West, the car horn is the prelude to serious road rage. I've seen people get out of their vehicles ready to rumble.

Not so here. After the honking is over, so is the issue. In a very Zen kind of way, the trouble is left behind and only the road ahead matters.

The last device Chinese motorists need is the musical car horn, the ones that play Dixie or the Superman theme. It will ruin everything.

Considering the Chinese love for musical mobile phone ring tones, there is no doubt some get-rich-quick clown can see the musical honking potential and is making plans.

It seems so many people are looking for the great beep forward.

PATRICK WHITELEY

(Jan 11, 2007)

23. **Driven mad in a cab**

The country's cabbies drive me crazy — in a good way, that is. Surely, some of the zaniest people I've met in China were behind the wheels of cars for hire.

There was the guy in Tianjin who clucked like a chicken at us for most of the trip. We never actually found out why.

Then there was the guy in Hainan who imitated what English sounded like to him — again, much like chicken clucking but with more consonant sounds — for a really, really long time.

An Australian friend and colleague tells me about the grabby cabbie who gripped his thigh and didn't let go. Instead, he jiggled it.

At first, the foreigner played along and even laughed. But as the cab driver kept holding on, his patience wore thinner and the situation made him feel increasingly touchy.

He patted the cabbie's hand to indicate that was enough. And when that didn't work, he gently seized the misplaced mitt, lifted it from his knee and re-deposited it on the driver's side of the vehicle.

Anyone who has spent a while in China has likely gotten a lift from a driver who seems keen to show off their musical tastes and talents.

My girlfriend and I got a kick out of one cabbie who picked us up, then cranked up the Eminem. My aforementioned friend and colleague also tells of the driver with the "pimped out" cab — fuzzy dice, leather seat covers and a racing steering wheel — who bopped to Backstreet Boys for their ride home.

But my favorite was the Kenny G-crooning cabbie who serenaded my girlfriend. He flashed her the CD cover and a toothy grin, and asked if she liked "Mr G". From the backseat, she responded with a sheepish "yes".

Carol hates Kenny G.

So he popped the king of sax in the player and started singing along. Because he didn't speak any English, he canorously adlibbed syllables that sounded similar to the lyrics in a deep voice. He did this the entire ride home, while casting enticing, eyebrow-raised glances at my girlfriend in the rearview mirror. Fortunately for me, she was somehow able to resist this driver's Siren songs.

On Sunday, I hailed a less-than-gabby cabbie. He shot down my attempts at language-exchange banter, so I hunkered down in the seat for what I expected to be a quiet ride home.

But when we hit a stoplight, he began rhythmically tapping his steering wheel in what was at first a fidgety way. However, within a few minutes, the tempo and volume picked up, and before long, he added the dashboard to his faux drum kit.

At that point, sitting still seemed awkward, so I decided to accompany him, slapping my knees and rapping the dash to the beat for the rest of the way.

Because of several setbacks that day, I was stomping mad when I hailed this drumming driver, but I disembarked with a cheerful bounce to my step.

I wonder if these crazy cabbies have any clue that for us, such unexpected experiences can make a bad day in the fast lane take an unexpected turn for the better — and for that, I'll sing their praises.

ERIK NILSSON
(Dec 9, 2007)

24. Getting a fix on happening Beijing

As the cultural capital of China, Beijing is simply bubbling with things to do and see. Art, music, sports — if it's a Chinese tradition, it will be practiced here. And if it's a Western trend, there will be a nascent scene.

Unfortunately, it's all too easy to miss out on the excitement by putting your feet up after a hard day's work and sticking in another DVD.

And so it was that I determined to try out something new by spending a couple of days with Beijing's fixed-wheel bike riders.

Fixed-wheel bikes are a type of ultra-cool personal transport made fashionable by cycle couriers in London, Tokyo and American cities. And now, Beijing has its own shop to supply the growing number of aficionados.

Owner Ines Brunn, a German trick-bike rider with sun-kissed blond hair and the kind of muscles I'd only seen on rock climbers, welcomed me inside for a cup of tea and a chat.

Apparently, China now has about 50 "fixies" — fans who prize the bikes for their minimalist beauty and individual style.

My host passed me a coffee table book full of glossy photos of fixeds that certainly had a retro charm I can imagine appealing to trendy urbanites who enjoy standing out from the crowd.

But it was with a nervous wobble that I rode off into the sunshine on my test ride, heading west into the maze of *hutong* on my borrowed steed, daring not to loosen my grip from the handlebars to give Ines a wave. I thought I heard chuckling.

Beijing's roads are crowded, noisy and jarring to the nerves, but its winding alleyways can be surprisingly quiet and peaceful.

Unlike my UK hometown, where pedestrians and drivers share an undisguised hatred of cyclists, Beijingers accept them as part of life and the *hutong* dwellers pulled their children out of my path with a warning — "*Che!*" (bike) — instead of giving me the evil eye.

The following day, I joined a group of about 40 riders by the ancient Drum and Bell towers. Xiao Shu (Little Tree), the owner of a nearby barbecued chicken wing shop, had traveled all the way to Guangzhou to purchase his bicycle — plus a smaller pink model for his girlfriend to ride alongside him.

Then we were off!

A gaggle of 40 riders completely blocking the road in both directions and arguing over which way to go — still without raising the hackles of the stymied motorists.

Riding in a pack is an enjoyable, almost primal, experience that unfortunately was cut short for me when I was left way behind.

Unlike my own cheap and clunky bicycle, fixes tend to be very light in weight, allowing faster speeds. It's possible the fitness of the riders also has something to do with it.

Pang Li

Under the glow of LEDs from the implausibly huge television screen at the shopping mall The Place, the riders played a game of bike polo.

Somewhat over-enthusiastic and shirtless throughout, Xiao Shu at one point careened right into a parked BMW with a sickening crunch. "Is the car alright?" was the first question asked.

The security guard watching the match quietly continued his observations, without raising an eyebrow.

I didn't try out bike polo myself. It looked far too dangerous.

But extreme sports seem ready to take off in Beijing, with ambitious plans underway for China's first extreme sports park. The park will surely be a magnet for the fixed gear crew, BMX riders and skateboarders. Young people will have a suitable place to go, away from precariously parked BMWs.

And at least they'll be out of those dreadful, gloomy Internet cafés.

DAVID DRAKEFORD

(Sep 24, 2009)

25. Changing gears on life's road

I got my bicycle ready early in the morning, and my 3-year-old son couldn't wait to hop on the small seat on the back.

As we passed the security guard, the boy uttered a complicated sentence that surprised us both: "Our car is even-numbered, and we can't get onto the road. If the police uncles catch us, they will fine my Mum."

Yes, our car has "0" at the end of the license plate, and we have to find an alternative way to send junior to kindergarten as the city enforces an even-odd license plate number restriction for cars around the Olympics.

The wind was pleasantly cool as the trees sheltered us before we reached the main road. When I'm driving, I always complain about how stuffy it is in the car, and my husband would advise me against turning on the air-conditioning too often. "It wastes gas, makes you sick and depletes the ozone layer," he'd say.

As I pedaled along, I realized that nature does a far superior job to any air-conditioner. I'm genuinely happy at our humble contribution to mother Earth's everlasting youth and vitality.

I grinned as my son kept exclaiming about the blossoming roses, the trucks carrying new cars and an auntie who covered her face with a huge hat with a broad transparent rim to serve as sunglasses. The ride gave us ample time to study the passengers, buildings and everything else that I had ignored as a focused driver.

My memory drifted back to the 1970s, when our family used to go for enjoyable rides on our loyal old bike. It was a Forever (Yongjiu) brand. It was the most valued member of the family, and it was 5 years older than me.

Every Sunday, Dad would take Mum, my sister and me on the sturdy bike and head for a nearby resort with hot springs. Yunnan is a mountainous province and the asphalt road wound along the slopes. We constantly had to jump off to give Dad a push.

On top of the hill, we'd all get ready. My sister sat on the crossbeam in front of Dad, while Mum held me and sat on the back seat. In a moment, the whole family would sail triumphantly down the slope, shouting and laughing.

Bikes were introduced to Shanghai in the 1860s as toys for the rich and powerful. Although some Chinese businessmen made bikes in the 1930s, most components were imported. It wasn't until the 1950s that China began producing its own. Forever, Pigeon (Fei Ge) and a few others were the most famous brands.

The bike beloved among Chinese farmers was nicknamed "the little donkey that doesn't eat grass". In the 1980s, some farmers would buy a Forever bike before anything else after a bumper harvest.

All this has changed over the last decade or so, as millions of Chinese families swapped two wheels for four. But I do hope the temporary restriction on cars reminds people how pleasant life can be without them.

As we turned into the path leading to the kindergarten, my son asked: "Mum, will you be tired, riding in the morning and afternoon for me?"

How could I be, my dear?

LIU JUN
(July 24, 2008)

4. CHEW ON THIS

26. Serving up the table talk

There was a bowl right next to my plate, so I took the lid off to peer inside, wondering what exotic food might be in store.

Inside I saw nothing. Absolutely nothing. This intrigued me because I knew a liquid was essential to cooking "hot pot" (*huoguo*).

I also had high expectations because every person with whom I had discussed Chinese food had asked if I had tried "hot pot". When I shook my head, it usually prompted a waving of hands, sighs, a rolling of eyes and sometimes a rubbing of stomachs, as the speakers described the delights of this yet unknown dish.

In any case, the moment to sample "hot pot" had arrived. We had carefully examined menus with beautiful pictures, which provided more information about the Chinese characters displayed on the page. A moment of enlightenment! The entire meal, broth and all, would arrive together. We chose our ingredients excitedly.

When it arrived, the "hot pot" was a slightly spicy liquid in a giant bowl surrounded by various raw wonders. In the center of our table was a lazy Susan where all the raw food was placed.

The lamb and beef had been rolled on a tray with meticulous care, while a garden of mushrooms standing upright in tofu was much admired and provoked many photographs. A tray piled high with miscellaneous greens, a bowl of noodles, a plate with sheets of dried tofu and another with shrimp were also squeezed into the last remaining spaces on the turntable. The liquid was ladled into our bowls, which sat on top of individual heating elements.

After the spicy liquid came to a boil, we began "the dance".

At least, it seemed a sort of dance, as we spun the food back and forth on the lazy Susan, waiting when others were reaching for certain items and learning to observe where others might be in their eating cycle so that you could turn the turntable to their advantage. I knew who had not sampled a particular food, and I also learned which foods were favorites.

It occurred to me that the dance was teaching us how to be more considerate of each other. In being more aware of my friends' immediate food needs, I waited to spin a different food closer to me. Even more, with every spin of the lazy Susan, my meal experience was more closely linked to that of my friends.

The moments of our meal were more richly experienced because, in the awareness of my friends' choices and methods of eating, I somehow learned more about them. They somehow became more familiar, their way of being more "known". I also wondered if this sharing gave them equal insight into my way of being?

And I also wondered if I had just stumbled upon one of the most worthwhile lessons to be learned in China: In learning to create a meal together, we learned a bit more about what it means to share life.

JANE HANSON
(Aug 6, 2008)

27. When Beijing sounds out

Every morning at 6:30, a man passes by our place, yelling something like, "Paperbackwriterrrrryahhh". The ritual is repeated three times throughout the day.

I'm told he is actually announcing that he has gas for sale, and I soon learned that it is a fine tradition in China to have people calling out their services or the wares they have for sale. After so much modernization, these voices are a link to life from long ago.

Compared to other forms of noise pollution, I do like this bit of pre-modern China.

Construction projects start as the sun is rising. Horns honk madly and constantly. People scream at children and even converse in shrieking tones while standing right next to each other.

Dogs bark incessantly. The vendors shout out. In stores, people bellow from one end to the other. Those wretched car alarms go off willy-nilly, and no one seems to heed them.

Restaurants are unbelievably noisy by Western standards. It is great fun when I take a friend to a favorite restaurant at about 5:45 pm.

My friend is invariably astounded at the staffers lined up stiffly in front while the manager paces back and forth giving instructions and trying to boost morale.

We sit down, the only ones there, and order. At 6 pm the tide of diners rushes in. Within minutes my guest is wide-eyed with wonder at the volume.

Chairs scrape loudly, orders are shouted back and forth, dishes clatter, children run around, men light cigarettes, several diners are shouting into mobile phones, and my friends ask: "Why is everybody so angry?"

I assure them no one is angry. They're just talking. In fact, if you look, you will see many of them are laughing — loudly.

This is the wild and wonderful scene at almost every Chinese restaurant. And if you don't let it bother you, dear foreigner, you will enjoy the liveliness of it all. But it does take some getting used to.

There are other forms of noise that I can't get acclimate to. I dread having a neighbor in the village die — not because I know the deceased, but, in this village, that means three days and nights of non-stop fireworks, drums and horns and processions to wail about the loss.

Then there are the fireworks necessary to mark the many special occasions. The ones I hate the most are those that only have sound and make me think someone is shooting a cannon. However, even the lovely sky-blossoms lose their charm after 10 pm.

All that pales in comparison to the latest entry in the noise sweepstakes. The other day we heard the dreaded sound of the weed-eater. This handheld device is like a mini mower that can get under bushes and into other tiny spaces where a mower cannot go.

Our gardeners, however, have decided to ditch the mower, which is admittedly noisy but does the job fairly quickly, in favor of this new toy. The circumference of this fiendishly loud device-from-hell is about 30 cm. We have a small grassy area, but cutting it 30 cm at a time takes hours — and hours. All day, in fact.

Headaches abound. Concentration disappears. Teachers have to shout.

Night shift people who are trying to sleep hang out of the windows,

begging for mercy.

Since part of my job includes a catchall called "Teacher's Services", my phone rings nonstop. What can I do about it? Apparently nothing, besides hoping we have very slow-growing grass.

SANDRA LEE
(Nov 17, 2009)

28. Meetings with famous meats

Sooner or later in the making of a new Chinese acquaintance, I will have to start a conversation about Kentucky Fried Chicken.

This is not an option for me; I have to do it. Not because I must express my fervent love for all eleven of their herbs and spices, and not because I'm being compensated for word-of-mouth advertising; it's because inevitably my new Chinese friend will ask the following question:

"Where in America are you from?"

I will then reply that I am from Kentucky. Kentaji.

Nine times out of 10, this is not enough. I don't blame him/her for not knowing, by the way. Most Americans would probably think Zhejiang, a souhern province, is a cymbal manufacturer.

"Maybe you've heard of KFC?" Kendeji. I only need to change one syllable in the name, yet the difference is huge. Everyone from taxi drivers to college professors knows the man in the white suit with the white hair and the white beard on the big red sign. "Oh! KFC! Your home is the home of KFC!"

Though I happen to be indifferent on the subject, I think many Kentuckians would be a little disappointed to learn that a greasy paper bucket of chicken parts is our only notable export to a fifth of the human population.

"What about the Kentucky Derby, the world's premier horse racing

Li Min

event?" some might object.

"What about our seven-time national championship winning college basketball team?" sports fans would protest.

"What about that one time our governor's plane caused an evacuation of the Capitol building because the transponder failed and everyone on the ground thought it was a terrorist attack?" people like me would say. "Wasn't that hilarious?"

"I'm sorry," interrupt the 2 million daily Chinese consumers of KFC food products. "Were you talking just now? I couldn't hear you over the sound of all these chicken sandwiches we're eating. What's the name of your state again?"

It's hard to argue with success. In China, KFC is actually growing faster than McDonald's, still the reigning champion of fast food in the States. One factor may be the wide variety of KFC products catering to the Chinese palate: congee, *youtiao*, egg tarts, to name a few. Or perhaps the real decider, the meat of the issue (if you will), is the meat. Despite the fact that you can eat chicken at McDonald's and beef at KFC, maybe the mental association with the vice-versa configuration is too strong. Rock beats scissors, scissors beat chicken, and in China, chicken beats beef.

Or could it be thanks to the comforting omnipresence of Colonel Harland Sanders, the man who started it all? I'm willing to believe that the Colonel's cross-cultural success was in the bag once his hair started turning gray. Respect for one's elders has long been a tenet of traditional Chinese values and I wouldn't be surprised if that plays a significant role in the popularity of KFC's official mascot/spokesperson, at least compared to Ronald McDonald. I haven't finished the *Analects* yet, but I'm pretty sure that clowns rank lower than grandfathers in Confucian hierarchy.

So where does that leave me? Until my kindly old ghost haunts 900 locations across China, I'll continue to live in the Colonel's shadow. And until China suddenly develops a taste for thoroughbred horse breeding or bluegrass music, it looks like my fellow Kentuckians and I will continue to live in the same place German expats from Hamburg have been living since McDonald's first landed on Chinese shores: in the shadow of a giant slab of meat.

GUS TATE
(May 27, 2010)

29. Steeped in culture, table talk brews

Hidden in a hard-to-find alleyway just down the road from Beijing's bustling Wudaokou subway station is a tiny teahouse. I'd seen the sign several times and suggested my friend Andrew that we swing in and check the place out.

We walked through the plastic curtain and entered the small room. A wrinkled old man was hunched over a small table set with clay teapots and a big, tea-pouring plate. His eyes were closed. He was sound asleep.

Inside, the air was hot and smelled strongly of tea — the raw, pungent, earthy smell of high-grade leaves. The room was sparse and clean. In one corner, a silent TV flashed American cartoons. In another was a small rocking chair.

Behind the sleeping man was a bookshelf filled with round wheels of *pu'er* tea, small tea sets and big tins of green tea. We tried to be quiet, but the man woke up and welcomed us into his home.

He jumped to his feet, grabbed a metal pot, filled it with water from a 10-gallon dispenser and set the pot on a hot plate. He waved us over to the tea display and talked enthusiastically, in rapid Chinese, about his stock. He laughed, cupped samples from various tins and invited us to smell the tea. It was fragrant and fresh.

While he spoke to us, we simply shook our heads knowingly and smiled. He didn't expect replies, but I tried my best to fire back a little Chinese to let him know his show was appreciated.

For a full hour, we sat across the table from the old man, sipping his tea and laughing at his stories. He told us about his hometown in Henan province, the dietary habits of his nephews and his experience with the weather in Beijing.

He'd lived in the big city for four years, he said, and he hadn't seen the stars yet. What a pity the pollution is. There are more foreigners here than ever before.

Basketball is OK to watch, but the players run too fast. The action is rapid, and the strategy is ad-hoc. That's why he prefers mahjong and chess.

Our cups were never empty. Immediately after we had drained the tiny glass bowls, he poured more. He laughed at our emphatic thanks after every refill and was impressed by our taste for his strong brew. As long as we kept drinking, he would have kept telling us tales and topping our cups. Until midnight, if that's what it took to quench our Western thirsts.

Eventually, I had to find an excuse for us to leave. I told him we had a meeting to attend at our campus. He shook his head and asked us to indulge in one more cup. We politely accepted.

I got up and picked up a glass bottle with a built-in tea infuser that I had spotted earlier. I asked him how much it cost. He said 20 yuan ($2.90). It was easily worth 50.

Andrew picked out some *pu'er* tea. He bought 20 yuan worth of the most celebrated variety. We paid, offered our sincerest thank-yous and promised to come back soon.

The old man saw us to his door, called us his American friends and told us to invite our classmates next time. He loved to meet foreigners, and on hot days like today he enjoyed the company.

NICHOLAS COMPTON

(Sep 4, 2008)

30. Smoke in mirrors

Many expats say China is a smoker's heaven and a quitter's hell.

A halo of smoke hovers above most friendly male-to-male interactions. And sometimes, refusing to light up can damn a guest to a most undesirable loss of face.

Packets of cigarettes are common gifts for participants of *fangwen* (official visits), and hosts are particularly keen to load up out-of-town visitors with local brands.

I was recently on a *fangwen* along with a non-smoker, who found it impossible to refuse a gift of top-brand cigarettes. The VIPs handed them over with a grin and a nod.

My poor pink-lunged friend accepted the offerings with a reciprocal smile and a dip of the chin, and puffed away.

He later lamented: "You can't get away with not smoking in certain circles in China." It's the exact opposite in the United States, where you can't get away with smoking in certain circles.

An American friend, who lives in San Diego, told me recently she quit because she found herself always looking for an excuse to get out of social situations to get that nicotine fix.

According to 2007 figures from the World Health Organization, China is the No 1 consumer of tobacco products in the world. About 60 percent of men and 3 percent of women smoke.

The figure for American smokers dropped to less than 20 percent this year, according to the US Centers for Disease Control and Prevention. In my hometown of Midland, Michigan, smoking has been outlawed practically everywhere aside from one's own home. There is no smoking within 8 m of any public building, meaning I can't even light up in the middle of the street.

When I took my brother to register for college last year, the policy had changed so that tobacco, including smokeless forms, such as chew, wasn't even allowed on campus at all under penalty of a fine.

In the US, and most of the rest of the West, smokers are viewed as black-lunged black sheep. But for men in certain situations in China, refusing to

Luo Jie

light up can extinguish a good rapport.

That's not to say one can never refuse. Most of the time, it's quite acceptable to decline. It depends on the situation and host.

Here, a cigarette is a unit of social currency. Its brand is a status symbol, and offering one to another person is a handshake, a smile, a toast and a pat on the back, all rolled into one and waiting for a match to be struck.

Before coming to China, I was at a personal record low of three a day. In university, I had been puffing more than two packs daily. After arriving in Beijing, that progress went up in smoke the first time I sat down at a table with a gracious host, who filled me with as much food, alcohol and nicotine as I could take — and then gave me some more.

I came close to quitting again earlier this year when I was bedridden with an excruciating cough, which caused my entire respiratory system to sting with searing pangs. It made me think of how much suffering the respiratory diseases my smoking might cause later in life, and I vowed to quit.

But my resolve was quickly foregone when I left my bed for a world of cheap, convenient and socially acceptable smoking.

Frankly, after that, I, like many people, had resigned myself to the notion that it was impossible to quit while living here.

But having seen many friends kick the habit in recent weeks, I've come to realize this was just another excuse to justify not doing so.

People, such as me, who are keen to quit while living in China, need to realize the fact that smoking is all too easy and this is the biggest obstacle.

After that, we just need to work through the thousands of other excuses but ultimately realize people — not the countries in which they live — make their own heavens and hells.

ERIK NILSSON
(Dec 9, 2008)

31. Superstition makes for hairy experience

I'm not a superstitious person but recently found myself following folk beliefs unwittingly — by getting my hair cut on the second day of the second month of the Chinese lunar calendar, which fell on March 20 this year.

There is a belief in China, particularly in the North, that forbids one from getting a trim in the first month of the Chinese lunar calendar, as doing so will bring a fatal curse on one's uncle.

In line with this belief, people usually put up with their long hair until the second day of the second month, known as "the day the dragon raises its head", symbolizing the coming of rain or an abundant spring.

It is believed that getting a haircut on this day will bring good luck in the new year.

Although I don't have an uncle, I did keep my hair until this day. But I didn't expect that so many others would do so, too.

I made an appointment with my hairstylist for 8 pm. I got there on time but found that he was still busy with the previous customer. I've never seen a hair salon filled with so many people. All eight chairs were occupied, and all three stylists were busy snipping away, with hordes of others patiently waiting their turn.

It was already half past 8 when my turn came. "You are my 16th customer today," my hairstylist Qin said.

Before he started with me, he kept exercising his fingers, adding that four more customers were expected later. "I'm not sure when I'll able to leave the shop — maybe after midnight," he said. He was yet to eat dinner.

Qin had started the day at 10 in the morning and had only managed a 15-minute break for lunch. That meant he had worked continuously for more than 10 hours.

"If you had not made an appointment, you would have missed the lucky day," he joked.

According to Qin, the day is always among the year's busiest. I saw several people come in looking for service, but all were turned away for lack of an appointment. They looked quite disappointed.

Lucky me!

I found out later that most hair salons and barbershops in Beijing were crowded with people that day. At the Silian Barbershop, one of the largest and oldest of its kind in the city, its 60 barbers had started work at 7 am. But they still couldn't meet the demand.

Many unlicensed barbers in *hutong* and old community areas also enjoyed very good business.

When I came into the office the next day, one of my colleagues noticed my hair.

"Finally, you got your haircut," she said. "You really are superstitious."

Well, let me just say, another of my colleagues who decided tradition was not for him, got his punishment — his new hairstyle is really weird!

LIN JINGHUA
(March 22, 2007)

32. Surgical precision at the hospital

Beijing veers from smooth efficiency one minute to sheer chaos the next. Every time I do something new, there's an added element of unpredictability, because I don't know whether things will be organized with military precision or whether no one will have a clue what's going on.

Take getting around the city. Look at a map of Beijing and you see an organized grid-style road network.

But when you undertake an excursion, chaos ensues. Crossing a road is like running a gauntlet. Bikes, cars, minivans, and even the odd horse and cart compete for space. People yell at one another, and cars constantly beep their horns.

Another battleground is the supermarket. Queues are an alien concept. I stand politely waiting to pay for my goods, and a withered old man is suddenly in front of me paying for his. I have to stop daydreaming and focus on the competition at hand, even if that means fending off the elderly.

But it seems the city is as good at clinical efficiency as it is at disorganization. I noticed this when I recently went to undertake the medical examination all foreigners have to undergo when they come to China with a Z (business) visa.

The HR lady at our company took me to the hospital. The test took

Li Min

place in a big hall with numbered rooms along the sides. It was bustling with foreigners, who were standing in long queues in every room and at the front desk. There were a few rows of tables where I sat to fill in the form, which I picked up from a clearly labeled desk.

Once the paper was signed, I had to visit every room to have various checks done. I was impressed at how thorough the test was. I had my eyes checked, my lungs X-rayed, my blood pressure taken, and was weighed and measured. I even had my blood extracted and an ultrasound scan.

Every test was carried out with such rapidity that I barely had time to register what was happening.

In the height/weight room, I was ushered onto a raised platform, and ushered off and out of the room within seconds.

For my eye checkup, I only had time to figure out that I was supposed to tell the direction of the symbols on a lit box about 4 meters away before I was whisked to the second part of the test.

For the ultrasound test, the nurse ordered me to lie on the bed and lift up my shirt. She then proceeded to smear cold jelly on my tummy and sides with a cold metal applicator, which made me wince. She peered at a screen in front of her, assessing my insides. I wondered how many other people had spent their morning looking at the internal organs of hundreds of people.

"Ok?" I asked. "Normal," she declared, before patting me on the shoulder in a signal to wipe myself off and leave.

The only hiccup occurred when I had my blood taken. Luckily, the pace of events slowed somewhat as the nurse tried digging a needle into my arm. However, even though she took a little more time than the other doctors and nurses, she couldn't quite get it right. Eventually, enough vials were filled, but I left the room with plasters on both arms and bruises.

When I was done, most of the rooms had cleared, and the nurses and doctors began to emerge from their stations for a well-earned break. I felt I needed a rest, too, as I was so taken aback by the sheer efficiency of the whole operation.

RACHEL O'NEILL
(March 25, 2010)

33. Facing the music

After spending more than three years in China doing everything I can to avoid karaoke, I realize it's time to face the music.

I hate singing but can't escape it. So, I have no choice but to change my tune and embrace the microphone, which somehow always ends up in my hand.

KTV follows me no matter where I go in the country. The full scope of its godlike omnipresence became apparent to me during a recent trip to Yinhu Cave in Beijing's northern suburbs. Set up amid the techni-colored stalactites and stalagmites of a yawning expanse in the subterranean tunnel were flashing string lights, a projector screen and a microphone.

The voice of a woman crooning pop anthems boomed throughout the chambers of this underworld cavity, as her friends whooped cheers from rows of seats bolted into the rock. While it undermined the Hades-like otherworldliness of the place, it created another. Even several km underground, there's no eluding this musical pastime.

A few days later, my family and I booked suspiciously affordable rooms at a hotel in downtown Guilin. After the sun went down, the volume went up at the karaoke bar across the street. Until the wee hours of predawn, a high-decibel cacophony created by a slew of amateur balladeers permeated our closed windows and our dreams.

But when it comes to karaoke, I don't mind being in front of the speakers. It's being behind the microphone that I abhor.

Somehow, I always end up having to croon for a crowd when I socialize with new people. In addition to being coaxed into KTV rooms during business trips, I've warbled Western tunes at banquets, when staffers wheel out the KTV setup after clearing the plates.

I've joined rousing sing-a-longs on buses equipped with sound systems. And I've choked out *Jingle Bells* to the accompaniment of an accordion in a Bouyei ethnic minority village's central square.

Since there is no means of polite refusal, I'm officially adopting an "if you can't beat 'em, join 'em" approach.

Having often been stumped when put on the spot with the demand to "sing us an English song", I've chosen the old British folk tune *I've Got Six Pence* as a stock fallback.

I settled on this after I was asked to serenade a table of government types and couldn't think of anything other than *Show Me the Way to Go Home*.

When I started belting out this little ditty, I realized they might misconstrue its meaning, believing my selection hinted that I longed to return to my chilly Beijing apartment rather than enjoying their warm Hubei hospitality.

So I was careful when later

Pang Li

83

interpreting into Chinese the song's gist, aside from the final phrase — "My mother's mustache!" They loved that part.

But I have a bigger problem in actual KTV establishments, because I honestly don't know the lyrics to a single mainstream Western refrain. Really.

A longer-term goal is learning a Chinese pop song. Right now, the only aria I can sing in Chinese is *Liang Zhi Laohu* (*Two Tigers*). This Mandarin kids' song shares the melody of *Are You Sleeping*.

But it's thematically different in that it's about two sprinting tigers — one has no tail while the other lacks eyes — rather than a dozing priest. I can also sing the French version, *Frère Jacques*, which comprises about 95 percent of the French I know. Doing so stretches the song out and makes it trilingual — a boon for sounding less stupid when you're a 26-year-old singing musical nursery rhymes to adults, and doing so off key while slaughtering the pronunciation.

By now, I'm certain it's impossible to lie low and sing small in China, so I have no choice but to tune in to the KTV culture of this harmonious society.

ERIK NILSSON
(Dec 1, 2009)

34. Now, KTV's music to my ears

I find it strangely refreshing that I am enjoying KTV.

Not that I dislike singing. On the contrary, I was an avid fan of pop music as a teenager. Never shy of acting differently from others, I would always belt out dance or rock songs at school singing competitions in front of all the straight-faced teachers who were learning to refrain from labeling the genres as "spiritual pollution".

But when karaoke arrived in my hometown in the late 1980s, even though I spent hours practicing singing and dance moves in front of mirrors, I found it distasteful.

It spread like a plague. Every restaurant, even the small hotpot stall, had a karaoke machine blaring all day long. The singers were usually tuneless, and their efforts sounded like screeching tires. Then, my parents' generation flocked to the microphone, yelling old songs.

Karaoke was for people to butcher pop, I decided.

Upon arrival in the United States, I found the singing environment much more orderly. On campus, there were a capella groups, rock bands and classical orchestras. But in that environment, I stopped singing.

One of my American lab mates invited me to a performance of his a capella group. Any one of them could have been a pop star in China, I

Pang Li

concluded. I declined his invitation to join, too chicken to admit I couldn't read music.

Then, karaoke seemed to pick up in popularity over there. I chanced upon a couple of karaoke nights at bars where the singers, some with huge beer bellies but all singing beautifully, could have advanced to the finals of *American Idol*.

Finally, one night in 2003, I gathered up my courage and stepped in front of a machine. I asked for the only English song I thought I could sing, and it went disastrously wrong. The key was too high and my vocal cords were tight.

I swore off karaoke after that humiliation, even though everyone at the bar applauded my effort.

When I returned to Beijing in 2004, I often found myself ending up at KTVs when there was a work or birthday party. When I suggested, instead, a fancy bar or club, my colleagues and friends would stare blankly and say they were boring.

Most of the time, I was lost at the KTV, having learned no Chinese pop songs in the previous decade. Gradually, however, the KTV atmosphere grew on me. I started to learn the new pop songs and enjoy the silly drinking games, which are designed to leave one with a huge hangover the next morning.

It was at a recent teambuilding event held at a KTV when I had an epiphany. Looking around the huge room, I saw my 30-plus colleagues happily chatting, drinking and fighting for the mic to sing cheesy ballads. It was then that I realized such a scene could not have happened in corporate America. There were female staffers giggling together like high school friends. Fathers and mothers were hanging out with colleagues, leaving kids to the care of grandparents. And blushing engineers were being dragged in front of the TV screen to sing.

It was then that I realized KTV's draw was not just about singing but, rather, a Chinese way of sharing time and camaraderie with people with whom one does not have to share life's intimate details to feel close. So, I went merrily along with the flow, and drank, sang and danced until the expensive bill hit me and made my head ache.

XIAO HAO
(Dec 10, 2009)

35. Dude, where's my phone?

The Guangzhou businessman was to the point.

"I'm not stealing your phone," he assured me. "I'm just not giving it back."

Behold the power of semantics. But still, his politician-esque assurances about my mobile had a very hollow ring.

My girlfriend had discovered something was amiss when she called me earlier that day. After a few redials, she came to realize that either I'd mastered perfect *putonghua* overnight or somebody had nabbed my phone. When she told me about it and found my Chinese was as atrocious as ever, we realized what had happened.

Upon calling the phone's surrogate owner, we learned that he had retrieved my mobile from the backseat of the cab on which we'd ridden the night before.

My 300-yuan ($40) blower was the cheapest available, but its phonebook contained an invaluable list of contacts whom I had no other means of reaching. We all know the hassle of finding and punching in all those numbers again.

So, I offered this Guangzhou businessman relatively big bucks to return my forlorn phone.

No dice.

What could I do? With nine-tenths of the law on his side, the guy with my mobile was definitely calling the shots — and anybody he liked, on my phone.

This episode wasn't the last bit of phone-related funny business I've encountered in China.

A few weeks later, I became something of a TV celebrity and poster child for what not to do when somebody begs to borrow your blower.

En route to picking up visiting friends from the airport, my girlfriend and I were accosted by a man who said he needed to make an emergency call. I lent him my new mobile, and all was fine until the guy got fidgety feet and began pacing away down the street.

I started pacing alongside him, ready to holler for help if he bolted.

He wrapped up his call and asked me if I had been worried. Kind of, but "it was cheap", I said — an answer blending honesty with politeness.

A few weeks later, a slew of texts and calls came my way revealing that my mug and mobile were plastered all over CCTV.

Apparently, I had been caught on candid camera! I'd been Punk'd, Chinese style! My hotfooted friend was making movies to educate the public about how to lend assistance to emergency callers while protecting your phone.

Last week, I lost my third mobile in a taxi and the crooked cabbie rendered me a loser and a weeper once more.

Since most of my Chinese friends have fantastically flash phones, I've come to understand the virtues of a sleek mobile and why these pals of mine prefer to dial with style. So, I bought a futuristic phone — cell phone No 4 — that would make Captain Picard jealous.

But the cacophony of bells and whistles that riddle this high-tech contraption confound me to the point of feeling more Amish than I ever have — something this Michigander never expected of his life in Beijing.

Captain's log: Star date July 4, 2007.

"As I continue to boldly go where few Michiganders have gone before, I have learned the value of giving my pocket the 'Have-I-got-my-mobile-phone slap test' upon disembarking from hired shuttles."

ERIK NILSSON

(July 4, 2007)

36. Buy, buy, buy, cell, cell, cell

My friend Wang Hui, like millions of her 20-something Chinese peers, recently spent her monthly salary on a mobile phone.

Wang works in a clothing market and makes 2,000 yuan ($263) a month. She thinks her new bells-and-whistles Nokia is the talk of the town.

It is a sleek-looking phone, but Wang tells me it can also take pictures, record videos, play music, has an alarm, a calendar, a personal planner, a world clock, a currency converter, blue tooth capability and a battery life of three days.

It also has the amazing ability to make a telephone call.

Wang is very, very happy and is probably feeling the same way many 20-somethings in the West feel after they book an overseas holiday, which costs them about one month's salary.

Twenty years ago, when China introduced its first mobile telecommunications equipment, there were little more than 700 users. In 2001, cell phone users passed the 100-million mark, and now China has more than 600 million mobile phones. This means that one in every five mobile phone users in the world is Chinese.

A mobile phone has become a serious status symbol, not only in China, but also all over our fast-consuming, materialistic world. However, in the

Middle Kingdom, an expensive mobile phone can give you instant status, no matter who you are. I've seen farmers on the Yangtze River chatting on smarter-looking mobile phones than those owned by Shanghai stockbrokers.

My friend Wang will be eating a lot of cheap noodles over the next month, but she insists her cell phone purchase was important and feels she has moved up in the world. She gives "upwardly mobile" a new meaning and cradles her new Nokia like a young mother holds a baby.

Another reason why there are 600 million mobile phones out there is because of forgetful people like me. I have lost three mobile phones in the back of Beijing taxis, and now I've changed my tune. To hell with the mobile phone fashionistas!

My latest Chinese-made phone cost less than 400 yuan ($53), and it's a little marvel. It is light, and when I drop it, it keeps on. I also like the compact look, the feel, the action and the catchy Mando pop ring tone.

But the best function for me is always the alarm. My little phone really is an eye opener. I've helped a lot of my friends from the West buy their first phone in China and have noticed many of them opt for the low-cost China-made communication solution. Maybe the back-to-basics attitude is catching on.

We have come a long way since the homing pigeon, and can you remember when the first mobiles arrived in the mid-1980s? They were so big, you had to carry them in a bag. And they cost about $5,000, so nobody really had one.

One of my first reporting jobs was to cover a major political convention. Our newspaper had been tipped off about the pending resignation of our state's long-serving premier. When the premier announced his retirement I had to rush to a payphone and call the editor.

A payphone? Now that's something we will be telling the grandkids.

PATRICK WHITELEY
(Sep 20, 2007)

II. CULTURE VULTURES

1. IN PLAIN LANGUAGE

37. Studying more to learn less

If you're a foreigner, I know your Chinese isn't very good.

In fact, it's probably horrible. Maybe it should even be described with expletives.

True or not, that's how you'll tell me it is. It's the universal response to the mention of a foreigner's Mandarin, whether you translate research on molecular biology or forget the word for "three".

Actually, I think your Chinese is great, and there's good reason you should, too.

Your declaration that your Chinese is dreadful is almost certainly heartfelt. Those with low levels usually know it. But those who have mastered some Mandarin find the more you learn, the more you realize you don't know.

So the better your Chinese gets, the worse you feel it is.

I spoke much better Chinese after studying for two months than after two years — at least it feels that way.

Most foreigners board a China-bound plane as adults and disembark as infants, in terms of communication abilities. I remember the day I regressed from age 22 to 2 during a single flight. When I stepped off the plane, I couldn't speak or understand what the "adults" were saying, let alone read or write.

From that point, everyone makes baby steps toward becoming toddlers

— linguistically speaking — able to communicate daily needs. Some continue developing into young children, and then teens, and a special few mature into adulthood.

But throughout the process, they feel their Chinese is dismal, with the adults feeling smaller and less mature than the toddlers. This exponentially growing inferiority complex is good in that it pushes foreigners to persist with *putonghua*. But it works the other way, too.

Self-criticism is perhaps the best source of self-improvement. But diving too deep and spending too long submerged in this well of inspiration for self-betterment can also drown one's spirit for it.

Many foreigners hell-bent on mastering Mandarin pull an Icarus, trying to

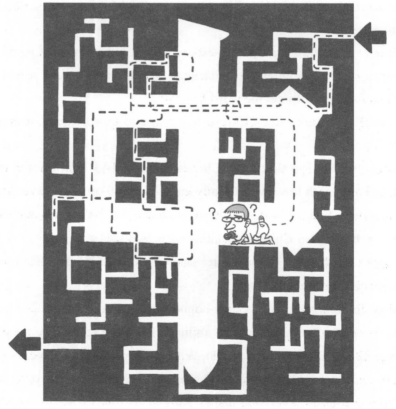

Luo Jie

fly too high too fast, getting burned and crashing.

Upon getting lost in the vastness of the language, which seems to grow with their proficiencies, they retreat to familiar territory — and stay there.

If Chinese people understand everything you're saying, that's terrific — and terrible. The good news is that you've reached a certain *putonghua* level. The bad news is that you're staying there.

I was delighted the first time I traveled with an all-Chinese group and everyone understood me. Then, I realized it was because I was relying on the same stock phrases.

A Chinese friend suggested I try some new words, and the head scratching began. Nobody had a clue what I was talking about — or trying to talk about, actually.

I wasn't feeling so delighted anymore. But leaving the tiny island that was my linguistic comfort zone meant that I eventually charted new territory within the language. Still, when I spend too much time outside my comfort zone, I start to feel really bad about my Chinese and itch to withdraw to familiar territory.

That's when my wife tells me that all foreigners speak great Mandarin. Her idea is that we should all periodically take a moment to feel good about our Chinese.

Those who take a break from bemoaning their pathetic *putonghua* will find it actually helps them stay the course. There's no light at the end of the tunnel that is Mandarin, so we'll all always be in the dark to some extent.

We must love and hate our wonderful, horrible Chinese.

So if you know any Mandarin at all, take a moment — right now's good — to pat yourself on the back for your *putonghua* progress.

You can use that same hand to beat yourself up over it later.

ERIK NILSSON
(June 16, 2009)

38. Competition makes me feel small

I protested as I was dragged toward the stage.

Yeah, I'd reluctantly agreed earlier in the evening to enter a Chinese-speaking competition at a party. But I hadn't signed up for the crazy scene that was about to unfold.

I had figured that I'd get walloped by some retired Sinologists who'd lived in China for several decades and did their PhDs on Tang Dynasty (AD618-907) poetry — and probably every other contestant of any ability, and thought: "Hey, what the heck?"

But as I was being hauled before the crowd, I saw what I was up against and immediately tried to escape the grip of the man leading me toward public humiliation — to no avail.

You could say it didn't take long to size up the other contestants. Not only was there little competition but also the competitors were all little.

I was pushed next to 12-year-old Ethan, who didn't even come up to my chest.

Next stood his 8-year-old brother, Nolan, who decided to join the contest for a bit of healthy sibling rivalry.

To his left stood 6-year-old David, with a very determined look on his face.

It wasn't clear whether the smallest tot, who looked about 2 or 3, was tossing her hat in the ring or not, because she kept wandering on and off the stage, as toddlers tend to do. I wondered if she could even speak at all yet.

I stood there, 1.83 meters tall, towering over my rivals like Goliath, wondering what kind of words David and his little friends were going to sling at me.

I stared into the crowd watching us, wondering what on earth these kids' parents were thinking.

They hadn't seen me get pushed onstage, nor had they heard my polite objections as I was dragged there.

All they saw was some goofy 26-year-old challenger dash in the middle of what had been a cute gathering of adorable little kiddies speaking Chinese in front of proud parents.

But there I was, spoiling this otherwise precious moment.

I gazed out at several hundred middle-aged family-types, crinkling disapproving foreheads at the stage — that is, at me for getting on it.

I just beamed at them with a grin that must have looked as dumb as I felt.

Only the event organizer, who'd talked me into signing up, smiled back.

She repeatedly jabbed her thumb into the air and bounced her chin in approval.

Since there was no escape, I figured I'd better just look on the bright side: At least I hadn't agreed to a basketball match.

I wasn't sure if it would be more embarrassing for me to win or lose. It almost didn't matter at this point.

The host started with little David — the toddler had wandered offstage again — who was asked to repeat: "*Ni hao*" (hello.)

Next, Nolan had to ask: "*Nihao ma*?" (How are you?) His big brother got: "*Wo hen hao, ni ne*?" (I'm fine, how are you?)

By the time my turn had come, I was wondering how you say: "I wish a

magical trapdoor would materialize beneath my feet", in Mandarin.

I was asked to repeat: "*Wei renmin fuwu*" (Serve the people.) And then the contest was over. While I'd lost my dignity, I won a thermos.

But the real prize from the experience was learning to make sure I know what I'm up against before entering any contest in China.

ERIK NILSSON

(July 7, 2009)

39. When babbling makes sense

The crazy guy sat alone on the park bench, babbling to himself.

He didn't notice the woman behind him. She watched him deliver an impassioned monologue, comprised of seemingly extraterrestrial utterances, to the evening air.

The woman likely thought he was speaking in tongues or in Klingon. Perhaps she thought he was another severely mentally ill citizen who had slipped through the holes in the United States' social safety net and landed in the park, where he likely also slept.

But none of these probable scenarios were true. That crazy man was me, practicing Chinese by speaking it to myself.

When I noticed the woman gaping at me, I wanted to explain what I was doing. But I realized that guys who sit in parks in small-town America speaking Mandarin to themselves aren't considered more normal than religious fanatics, sci-fi super geeks or the mentally ill.

Various versions of this scene have played out repeatedly over the following years, because I do find that chatting to myself in Mandarin really does sharpen my proficiency. And, lost in furious concentration, I often fail to notice when I'm suddenly not alone anymore.

In the US, strangers nary have a clue that I'm speaking Chinese, or a real

language at all. But I'm not sure I appear much saner when Chinese people catch me giving speeches to the air, in bad Mandarin, when I think I'm alone.

I've never asked anyone who has accidentally sneaked up on me practicing Chinese what he thinks of a foreigner sitting on a curb in the middle of the night trying to discuss the impacts of upcoming political reforms with a

Li Min

lamppost. And if I did ask, how could they even be sure I was talking to them?

But the method truly is effective. That's why it's the foundation of the English-instruction empire built by controversial entrepreneur Li Yang.

Li has largely based his lucrative language-instruction business on the unorthodox approach by which he taught himself English as a university student — that was, pacing in the courtyard of Lanzhou University, shouting English to the sky at the top of his lungs.

He had been worried about passing the College English Test, because he needed to qualify for Level 4 or higher to graduate, he told media. Reportedly, he earned the highest score on the exam in his department.

The brand name for his company: Crazy English. And many people believe Li is genuinely crazy. Some accuse him of running his business like a cult, doing things such as allegedly forcing young students to kowtow to him.

I'm not looking to be idolized by masses of bowing kids or making boatloads of cash. Really, I just want to improve my Mandarin.

And there are many perks to practicing Chinese by speaking it to myself. The greatest is that the degree of patience with which my audience tolerates my stumbling, mispronunciations and restarts is up to me, because, well, I am my audience — the entire audience, that is.

So, if it truly helps me elevate my linguistic aptitude, do you really think it's crazy to talk to oneself?

Don't answer that. I wasn't even talking to you.

ERIK NILSSON
(March 2, 2010)

40. Express route to my Mandarin misunderstandings

My cell phone lit up with a number I didn't recognize.

Numbers I don't recognize tend to belong to Chinese-speakers, so I prepared my best, tone-rising "Weeeii".

As I moved the phone toward my ear, I felt a rush of pride in my Chinese skills.

The embers of my pride in my *putonghua* roar daily with the praise of China's taxi drivers and fruit vendors, which means my ego has grown to the size of a small house pet.

On this warm night in Guangzhou, I had decided to take my giant ego for a walk with a friend of mine to Beijing Avenue — the pedestrian-only street flanked by a gaggle of lights and shops akin to Beijing's Wangfujing.

The mystery call wasn't in the plans, but I knew it was just another chance to flex my Chinese muscles.

"Weeeii?" I answered.

The mystery caller introduced himself: "Hey, I'm Kuai Di!"

My pulse quickened. I had no idea who this man was, but he clearly knew who I was. My mind raced for a strategy.

I knew "Kuai Di" was his name because Chinese names are usually two syllables. I racked my brains to think of where I had met someone named Kuai Di.

Cell phone numbers and business cards are given out as easily as hellos in China, so I've become accustomed to giving my cell phone number to people I'm sure have no intention of ever calling me. But now, I was being ambushed by someone who had decided to actually call.

After my brain racking failed to turn up any memorable Kuai Dis, I decided to pretend I knew who Kuai Di was and see if I could figure out who he was by prolonging the conversation. "Soooo ... Kuai Di! How have you been lately?"

"What? I'm Kuai Di. Kuai Di!"

"I know, I know! You didn't think I'd forget, did you? How have you been recently? *Hao jiu bu jian* — it's been so long since I've seen you!"

"I ... am ... Kuai ... Di. Kuai Di!"

"Don't be such a stranger! I know who you are, Kuai Di. So, how've you been?"

"What are you talking about? Listen! Is anyone home? I'm downstairs."

Now my embarrassment turned to fear. I was across town, and there was a man with a burning desire to repeat his own name — possibly with a mental illness — waiting outside my apartment, asking me if anyone was home.

Pang Li

Obviously, my time in China up to this point hadn't prepared me to handle mystery phone calls. But I had managed to learn from my students the art of the bald-faced "maybe".

The art is simple. Whenever asked a question you don't want to answer, just sprinkle a drawn-out "maybe" into any sentence that shouldn't have one.

Good teachers don't just teach; they learn from their students. As a good teacher now desperate for a Plan C, I brandished a bald-faced "maybe".

"Maaaybe someone's home. Why? What's up?"

"What!?" Kuai Di was at wit's end. "I'm Kuai Di! Kuaaai Diii!"

Exasperated, I handed my cell phone to my Chinese friend.

"He's trying to deliver a package to your place. I'll just tell him to leave it with the guard."

It turns out that "*kuai di*" is not a Chinese name. It means, "express delivery". In other words, I had unwittingly forced a poor Chinese deliveryman into an Abbot and Costello routine.

And so the waxing and waning of my Chinese ego goes. As soon as it reaches epic proportions, a debacle comes along to bring it down to size and remind me that my Chinese still has a long way to go.

On the upside, though, I guess this means that I can cross Food Delivery, Water Guy and Express Delivery off my Christmas shopping list.

THOMAS TALHELM

(Dec 15, 2009)

41. Discovering a language like Indiana Jones

Learning Chinese is like exploring a Raiders of the Lost Ark-type underground tomb. Fire lanterns hang on tunnel walls, and between each lighted area is frustrating darkness.

In the beginning, the Chinese beginner spends most of the time in the dark, and then wonderful moments of clarity light the path. The four tones actually start sounding different, new words learned weeks before leap to mind, and even some of those strange squiggly lines make sense. Then it's back along the dark trail of twisted sentence structures and *de* and *le* and *ne*.

Like Indiana Jones, I'm searching for treasure, and my Holy Grail is the Chinese language. I've been learning intensely for three months, and it has been one of the hardest and most interesting learning experiences in my life.

I'm deep in the cave, but I see a light. I know there is a long way to go, but the treasure is near. I'm starting to hear it on the streets, and see it on those big neon signs that light up Beijing.

Learning anything well always takes time, which seems to be the most valued commodity among China expats.

Time spent here and Chinese language ability — which is all about time — seem to sort out the expat pecking order, and the two attributes normally match one another. The longer the expat stays, the better the Chinese speaker.

There's something fair about all of this, because these treasures cannot be bought. They have to be earned.

Everybody has to do their time in the long, dark tunnel.

Speaking Chinese requires thousands of hours. Money can help buy the best teachers, but no matter how much an hour I spend on a super language instructor, I have to spend hours every day on my own, saying words, listening to tones and memorizing characters. There is no trick to studying, no secret method. I just have to do it.

My need-to-speak-Chinese turning point came after my first year. I had not progressed beyond 100 words and was sick of not knowing how to speak to 99.9 percent of the people here.

China had been so much fun up until that point. Most of my Chinese friends could speak English, and they explained how things worked. I could see it all in 3D, but I couldn't hear it for myself. It was all second-hand news.

Traveling around China made my isolation even worse. Every time I explored a different part of this beautiful country, my experience was always limited to mountain views, not points of view.

China isn't only about its breath-taking gorges, its serene mountains or its life-giving rivers. And it's certainly not about its expat bars.

China is about its people, and I couldn't hear the stories they were telling. Now, I am starting to hear and can understand a deeper level about the marvels of the Middle Kingdom. By the time the Olympics comes around, I will be able to speak Chinese if I keep searching in the darkness.

The other really cool bit about speaking Chinese is its long-term value. As China continues to rise, so will the opportunities for us foreign Chinese speakers. The treasure awaits all who venture in the tunnel.

PATRICK WHITELEY

(Sep 26, 2007)

42. More to language than just words

One of the best parts of studying Chinese in China is overhearing conversations between people who assume I can't understand them.

"Hey, check out the nose on that foreigner!" "Is he Russian?" "Ask him if he likes Chinese food." "No, you ask him!"

My fellow American teacher Jon and I try to be a little more careful when we're out and about in Guangzhou, usually sticking to rapid or colloquial English when referring to our fellow subway passengers. After last weekend, though, we're seriously considering taking up American Sign Language.

Jon and I bought tickets to a show in Shenzhen. To save money, we purchased through an online agency that provides two-way transportation.

Upon arriving at the bus pick-up point just on time, we were surprised to discover the event organizers handing out nametags. My heart sank.

I had been on Chinese tour buses like this before. I knew what was coming.

I turned to Jon. "We," I said, "may have to sing karaoke."

Sitting in our second-row seats as the bus prepared to depart, we noticed that our Chinese bus-mates were all about our age. Jon switched to French, a language we have both studied but can only pretend to speak fluently.

"Il faut faire attention; il y a beaucoup d'étudiants ici." ("We should be

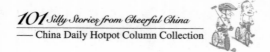

careful; there's a lot of students here.")

"Oui. Je suis d'accord. On ne parle pas l'anglais." ("Yes, I agree. Let's not use English.")

Feeling less like unwilling performers and more like secret agents, we decided to pretend that we spoke only French and could not comply with any requests to sing *Take Me Home Country Roads*.

We laughed haughtily, tweaking our imaginary mustaches and smoking imaginary cigarettes, attempting, with our limited vocabularies, to comment (loudly) on the hairstyles and possible romantic relationship of the couple sitting directly in front of us.

As the bus rolled away from the station, the group leader took the mike

Li Min

and spoke to the group in Chinese. "Hi guys! My name is Leaf! I want everyone to take turns introducing yourselves to the group; tell us what you do, where you're from, what your hobbies are."

She passed the mike to the woman in the first row. "Hi, everyone! You can call me Xiao Zhang, I'm from Guangzhou and I'm a French major at Sun Yat-sen University."

I slapped my forehead. Jon's imaginary cigarette fell out of his mouth.

The man in front of Jon spoke next: "Hi, guys; I'm Xiao Li. I live in Paris but I'm back in Guangzhou visiting my family."

Jon and I looked at each other, both of our faces now an embarrassing shade of rouge. Somehow we managed to stand up and bumble through our self-introductions without incident, but surely everyone in the back of the bus must have wondered: "Why were the foreigner's faces so red? The one on the right looked like a tomato."

Back in our seats, Jon and I tried to regroup.

"We could speak Pig Latin?"

"Ouyay eallyray antway otay eakspay ikelay isthay orfay otway hourshay?"

"Okay, maybe not."

Besides getting a lot of reading done that day, Jon and I also received a valuable reminder: English isn't the only foreign language in which Chinese students are interested. We never worked up the courage to apologize to the francophone couple. At least we succeeded in avoiding any requests for a serenade.

In any case, it looks like we'll need to work on our cultural ambassadorship — or, at least, our German.

GUS TATE
(May 5, 2010)

43. A hellish contest with Devil Judge

Last month, CCTV9 International screened the final of its annual English-speaking Cup. I had an interest in this academic version of *Super Girl*, co-staged by the Foreign Language Teaching and Research Press (FLTRP), having co-judged the penultimate round.

Nine of us had pared 92 semifinalists down to just 23 in three days of 5:30 am calls, butt-numbing judging sessions, sickly instant coffee and the pressure of knowing that our vote could make a difference.

It's a big deal. Former winners have won scholarships to Yale, joined debating contests at Oxford and gained places at top universities without needing to do the entrance examinations.

Presenter Liu Xin, the first Chinese person to win an international English-speaking contest (1996), became an anchor for CCTV.

Despite a great start by most of the students, the English often fell down once the prepared speeches were done. Performances became panicky, and there was a tendency to waffle rather than answer the questions.

Many mentioned the importance of Chinese culture but in a quiz section didn't know as much as I did about famous Chinese teas, or minority costumes, or even that a character depicted on the screen was the original form of today's *shui* (water).

While appreciating this irony, I was gaining myself quite a reputation.

After each contest, a large screen showed each judge's photograph and the marks they had awarded underneath. My score was usually the lowest of the panel.

I became Devil Judge.

The antipathy began with a reluctance to let me jump the toilet queues.

There were tears.

"I go to one of the best universities in China! I should have won! I should have scored at least 88!" cried a student whom I had pushed myself to award 80.

"You're giving high scores to all the rubbish ones and the good ones are just getting 70s!" claimed another.

And here was another irony. The lowest and the highest marks were disregarded, so often my scores didn't factor anyway.

One contestant singled me out to thank me. I had given him my top score, so he must have realized how highly I had ranked him.

It's a national competition, and we were there to sort the wheat from the chaff. (Points would have been available if someone had used that expression.) One's university is irrelevant.

A perfect American, or very occasionally British, accent isn't enough. Nor is a pretty, polysyllabic prepared speech. The contest tests the ability to engage an audience, not force them to watch the timer; the ability to fluently answer cruel questions flung from mean question masters; the maturity to deliver intelligent, grammatically sound answers to the actual questions asked. It's hard.

The contestants who didn't make the final, despite having many talents, simply didn't have enough, and if they had stood among the finalists they would have looked like fifth-graders.

The standard of those who did make it through was astonishing.

A native speaker could hardly have bettered the quality of English delivered in the debates and impromptu questioning.

When I tuned in on the final day, I saw the contestant to whom I had awarded my highest mark lift the cup.

At 19, Shi Yupeng, a biology major at Fudan University, was the youngest of the 23 finalists. The Fujian province native said his English came mainly from listening to CNN and BBC.

And to all those who were disappointed not to get to the final, please don't blame the ref. You were good, but you were battling China's very best.

DEBBIE MASON
(Dec 10, 2008)

2. YOU NAME IT

44. In the name of the emperor

It is the most important day of our lives, and we're too young to even know it.

I'm talking about the day our parents name us. From this day on, we could spend the rest of our lives being called Bill Ding (building) or Don Key (donkey) or Chris P. Bacon (crispy bacon). We put a tremendous amount of trust in our parents on this day.

But fear not, we get another chance when we study a different language or move to a foreign country.

It is a big moment in the life of a Westerner when he finally receives a Chinese name. It is the day he feels like he truly belongs in China. When you are a tall, goofy-looking *laowai*, it's difficult to blend in on Beijing's streets. But at least when you have a Chinese name, you feel like you have an identity, like a little part of you has become Chinese.

I used to teach at the University of Science and Technology, Beijing. While I was there, my boss gave me the name Fu Lin. Fu Lin, which is close to my surname of Coughlin, was also the name of a Chinese emperor who ruled in the 1600s. I thought this was a great name.

Think about it. One day I am Adam, a simple teacher, but the next day I am sharing a name with a Chinese emperor. I felt like I could conquer the world — or at least handle a class full of well-behaved Chinese students!

My friend Frank didn't have such good luck. His middle name is Newman and so his Chinese name is Niu Ben, which, when you write it in Chinese, looks like four cows. Frank says people always laugh at him when he tells them his Chinese name.

People always smile when they hear the name of my friend Eric. Eric moved from New York City to Beijing to work at a Chinese website. His coworkers were so excited that he came and thought he would help their company so much that they had an intense discussion about what an appropriate name for him would be.

However, the heated debate was in Chinese, so he didn't understand. Eventually, they narrowed it down to three choices: Beauty in the Autumn, Man of the People and The Future. They decided on Wei Lai or The Future. Needless to say, Eric thinks it is the coolest name in the world.

Max Quillen knows his Chinese name is common to everyone but him. He has lived in China for almost four years but was given his name, Lin Qiang, when he first arrived.

"I think it's a bit like John Smith (a generic Western name) in terms of commonness but with some heroic soldier-type connotations, which makes me feel tough. So I like it."

For all of you studying a foreign language, think long and hard about the name you want to have. William Shakespeare once wrote: "What is in a name? That which we call a rose by any other name would smell as sweet." This might be true for flowers, but names help define who we are. And you'd better listen to me. Remember, I am an emperor!

ADAM COUGHLIN
(April 23, 2008)

45. The name's Bong, James Bong

Juliet asked Romeo: "What's in a name?"

I go one step further: "What's in a surname?"

The name game in China is so full of information and mystique that even if you know Chinese, you'd be overwhelmed.

When I was a kid, I thought there were only 100 surnames in China, ignorant that *Hundred Family Surnames* could mean "countless unfamiliar ones not included". A typical surname is so untethered from the original meaning of the word that nobody named Wang (literally, King) would have any hint of royal supremacy. But it took on special connotation in the canon of revolutionary arts and literature.

When a "model" opera assumed Diao as the surname of its crafty villain, it basically summed up the character in one, well, character. And a classmate of mine with the same moniker was instantly turned into a target of peer derision.

I never thought of myself as a "week" since *zhou* the week and *zhou* the family name were written differently until our language was simplified in the 1950s. I was proud to share my name with Zhou Enlai, beloved premier of New China, not knowing how close he was to being toppled by the Gang of Four.

But the premier's high stature did not save me when a best-selling children's book came out. Its evil landlord forced his underage child laborers to work during the wee hours by forcing the rooster to crow before the set time. The baddie was named Zhou.

A friend, who is a language professor at Sun Yat-sen University in Guangzhou, can rattle off the last name of each character on television.

She is not a soap opera junkie but, rather, just knows the secret to christening fictional individuals by way of association. Many times, she hits it home, and, for those she misses, I have the feeling the aliases she coins are a better fit.

Today, if you don't like your given name, you can change it, but few would tinker with their family names. Even big-name writers with pen names, such as Ba Jin or Cao Yu, would still name their children after the original family names.

Turning back on your family roots is considered a disgrace. Thanks to the Internet, people can adopt and change their handles as frequently as they fancy while keeping the family label gloriously intact in real life.

So, when I met a "Fifth Element" recently, I assumed he was a big fan of Luc Besson. But no! That's his real name.

It can be traced back to the Three Kingdoms (AD 220-280), when a big family named Tian had to embark on an exodus. They divided into eight numerated units and scattered. Later, the other branches were all killed off, Fifth Element claimed. But I suspect they all secretly changed their names back to Tian.

Unless you are James Bond or a prisoner, you would not want to be identified only by a number — QQ numbers excepted.

Speaking of 007, a friend surnamed Pang took on the English name James. Now he introduces himself as James Bong. (Most Westerners read ang as ong, anyway.) A totally unrelated friend named Diao (crafty again) chose Christian as his English given name. So, now he is Christian Dior.

RAYMOND ZHOU

(Jan 16, 2007)

46. Rewriting the name game

The name game is played according to a totally different set of rules in China. Here, Chinese and foreigners get to choose their own appellations in each other's languages. But when people start making names for themselves outside of their mother tongues, the results are often comical to native speakers.

I've seen many foreign friends elicit guffaws from native Mandarin speakers when announcing their self-selected Chinese designations. However, this end of the equation is lost on me. And even after the Chinese would explain why these foreigners' names were so funny, those of us on the *laowai* side of things usually just couldn't quite get it.

I imagine it's the same thing in reverse for those names Chinese choose for themselves that native English speakers find amusing.

My girlfriend works as a Business English instructor at China Agricultural University, and her student roster provides some prime specimens of this phenomenon.

When Carol asked 11 how to spell his name, for example, he simply held up both index fingers. In 11's class, Rainbow sometimes sits between Sunny and Rain, who are in the same section as Weather. However, Shadow is, appropriately, in a different class than Sunny.

One of Carol's colleagues has Clean Water in her class, along with another student from last semester, Hotmail. She recalls the day Hotmail sat behind Clean

Water, and she confused the friends by accidentally calling on "Hot Water".

Hotmail says he chose his name because it was a phonetic approximation of his Chinese name, Hou Miao. When Carol had him last semester, his classmate also took a name brand for a namesake: Gucci.

When Carol was given a new class section last week, she got a few giggles out of her new roster, which lists the likes of Axl and Wheat. But Bingo — yes, Bingo really is his name-o — was her favorite pupil.

She got another laugh out of this batch when she first met Alansmith, because he insisted: "It's one word, but you can call me Alan." And you can also call Duckmonster Duckmon, if you'd like.

Upon starting lessons in that class, Carol quickly found that Dim's moniker is a misnomer, because he and his colorful classmate Neon are among her brightest pupils. And Smart, the 11-year-old Carol tutors, is also a clever kid who truly lives up to his name.

Sometimes, students select names based on qualities they aspire to. For example, Leader hopes to become a government official. But while Sin's pseudonym seems to extol evil as her most venerated virtue, she's actually quite nice. One of Carol's colleagues also has a student named Sin in the same section as Lucifer.

Like most foreigners, I've encountered several strange pseudonyms outside of Carol's classes. One of my first language-exchange partners was a bartender named Tiger, who took this title from the brand of beer. Because his English was scant, when explaining the meaning of his name, he would curl his fingers in front of his face, bare his teeth and let loose with a guttural growl. His colleague Mouse, however, was meeker in explaining his moniker.

The list of odd appellations goes on, and anything goes. And I do mean anything — you name it.

ERIK NILSSON
(Oct 31, 2007)

47. What's in a name, anyway?

The Year of the Pig is coming to an end, and many couples have had their babies, as planned. In China, people believe a child born this year will be lucky, prosperous and fertile.

I don't believe in this sort of thing. What I think is that newborn babies cause problems for their poor parents in many ways. They keep them up all night, for instance, and they are expensive to feed, clothe and educate.

The first problem parents usually encounter, however, is what to call these "little golden pigs".

Recently, I have received a lot of requests from my friends to help name their babies — so much so that I am thinking of opening a child-naming business.

Naming a baby was much easier in the past. For instance, in the good old days it used to be that if a baby was born with a bruise on his or her butt, he or she was simply called "black bottom".

In the early 1950s, thousands of Chinese people were called "Weiguo" (great country), or "Jianguo" (founding a country), or "Jianjun" (establishing an army) to celebrate the establishment of the People's Republic of China.

During the late 1960s, "Hong" (red), the color of the revolution, became a popular name for babies.

Nowadays, unusual names are fashionable, as parents want their child to be unique. Also, women don't want their surnames dropped and therefore add it to their husband's name.

As a result, children's names seem to have got longer. Double-barreled names are no longer rare in China, and I can't help thinking that one day Chinese people will have names as long as those of the Japanese.

Earlier this year, a Chongqing native tried to give his son a quadruple-barreled name —— Ouyangchenggong Fenfatuqiang. It sounds like a revolutionary slogan and was given in the hope that his baby would work hard for prosperity. His request, however, was turned down by the local registration office.

Another way to avoid the same name is to search the dictionary for something unusual.

Some parents haven't touched a dictionary since leaving school but pick them up again to find odd names for their babies. Of course, they are happy with their choices, but will it sound so good when the child has grown up a little and his or her teacher is calling out something odd in class? Won't there be jokes?

Besides dictionaries, the Internet has become popular among young parents for providing a lot more options, so they can choose a name like picking lottery numbers.

I feel sorry for my friends. In my eyes, success in life has more to do with working hard, ambition and determination rather than a great name. A person with a common name might have a prosperous life, while an auspicious name can be a burden.

I urge my friends to take it easy, but they don't listen.

"When you have your own child, I bet you will change your mind," one of my friends told me.

We'll see.

XIE FANG

(Nov 21, 2007)

3. LABORS OF LOVE

48. Getting married for the mob

They took off my glasses and gave me a gun.

Then, they handed me a wife — my fifth since coming to China and I've never been divorced.

The ceremony in which I was provided a firearm and a new bride wasn't a serious shotgun wedding — the weapon was actually a musket — but rather, a performance for tourists showcasing the marital customs of the Miao people in Guizhou province's Basha village.

The reason I've gotten hitched so many times since coming to this country is that I often find myself at the intersection of two cultural crossroads.

The first is that most ethnic minority villages reenact wedding ceremonies for guests and do so with crowd participation. The second is that many Chinese seem to love watching foreigners make fools of themselves on stage. And when I visit these settlements, I'm usually the only overseas guest.

My most recent nuptial began with my bride-to-be force-feeding me huge globs of mashed rice and ended with me doing the same to audience members.

Just months before that ceremony, I married an ethnic Yi woman in Guangxi Zhuang autonomous region's Longji Rice Terraces.

First, I was dressed in the ethnic group's traditional garb — a red head-wrap and a sash with a bow resembling those worn by beauty pageant contestants.

Next, I had to gulp several goblets of liquor with my arms interlocked with my soon-to-be wife's, while several old women pinched my buttocks — hard. The goal is not to spill the spirits, even though a gaggle of grannies are kneading your buns like dough. I'm very ticklish, and soon had a damp shirtfront and bride — and a sore derrière.

There's no way I can be sure, but I suspect this longstanding marital custom dates back to the vibrant time in the village's rich history when locals figured out that tourists would think such antics very funny to watch.

After getting goosed while tipping back tipple, I had to croon an English-

Li Min

language love song for the crowd.

I froze up.

All I could think of was *You Are My Sunshine*, and I began serenading my new partner and the spectators with this little ditty. But before long, I realized I only knew four lines of the ballad. The advantage of being about the only native English speaker is that nobody seemed to be any the wiser when I kept repeating the only part I knew to draw out the performance.

Suddenly, my bride hopped on my back and told me to run around the stadium.

So, I charged around the bleachers wearing the new missus like a backpack until we reached the exit, where several women stood with arms linked to block us.

It took several attempts to break through their barricade Red Rover-style, trying to use the extra momentum provided by my wife's weight combined with mine. Finally, I was backstage.

My actual wife, an American woman whose sense of humor exceeds that of her jealousy, was present for this show, as she was the first time I married an ethnic minority member, a Li girl in Hainan province's Binglanyuan.

That day, I had no idea what was going on when I was whisked into the hut — at least until after they'd dressed me in a red vest and flat cap, and a woman grabbed my hands and placed them on the back of her upper thighs. She instructed me to hoist her toward the roof beams so she could kiss a pair of beetle nuts slung from the rafters. My face turned the color of my crimson vest.

So did my American wife's. And then poor Carol started crying — from laughing so hard, that is.

ERIK NILSSON
(May 26, 2010)

49. The formula for love

For anyone banging his or her head against the wall in the world of dating, it seems the answer could lie in your calculator.

I recently spoke to Shanghai millionaire Dr Li Song, CEO and co-founder of the world's largest matchmaking website for Chinese speakers, www. zhenai.com.

With "*zhen ai*" meaning "true love", it boasts 23 million registered users. And new ones are signing up at a rate of 30,000 a day.

The key to Dr Li's company's matchmaking success? Some amazing intuition into how lovers feel, into how their hearts beat, what makes their tears flow?

Not at all. In fact, it all comes down to quantifiable statistics and probability.

The size of Dr Li's database enables his team of 400 call-center matchmakers to input the data for each new seeker of love, and out pops the most likely suitor for his or her profile.

Details, such as length and style of hair and clothes and manner of speaking, are all collected.

The matchmakers advise those who sign up that 70 percent of women with long, straight hair get second dates.

Just 5 percent of those with short, curly hair do.

His team advises women to wear above-the-knee skirts, high heels and definitely black, translucent pantyhose. "Not too low-cut for the tops. If you wear something too low-cut you lead a man to think of you in the wrong way. In other words you want to be sexy but not sexual," he stresses.

"We don't worry about being politically correct. We merely tell our clients what we have observed."

His observations, statistics and enormous database have produced some rather surprising findings.

"Despite the feminist argument in recent years, we find that women still care far more about profession, social status and income than looks," he says.

"Men are better off dressing as close to a business style as possible, but it's not the most important thing at all."

For the men, salary is barely important, but the women should be 27, either teachers or nurses, and 1.62 meters tall.

"There are two approaches to matchmaking," Li says.

"One is that you come up with a psychological theory and predict the results based on your theory, but because my background is more mathematically inclined, I don't have a theory to begin with.

"What I do is based on statistical results and reverse engineering, and is a learning process.

"We operate on two matrices: How many of our callers get at least one date — we aim for 93 percent — and the time it takes between establishing contact and the actual date. This should be within two and a half weeks."

So much for the language of poets — better speak equations, qualitative finance and probability if you want success in the romance department.

A former finance PhD student at Cornell, the bespectacled, mid-40s Li does look just like a mathematician.

There are no roses or chocolates in his very ordinary double room at

the Beijing International Hotel, and he wears a slightly marked, pale orange sweatshirt with baggy grayish slacks.

But despite his own shortcomings style wise, he knows the dress code for success.

He tells me I would be all wrong in my trousers, though the high heels are a good idea. And he admits that when he met his wife, she was wearing black pantyhose.

DEBBIE MASON
(March 10, 2010)

50. Till death do us part

When I told my Chinese friends I was getting married this May, they wrinkled their foreheads to resemble walnuts and vaulted their eyebrows into boomerangs.

"But you're so young!" they insisted.

When I told my foreign friends, they also spoke exclamatorily, making proclamations such as: "Ooh, congratulations!"

Age is among the slew of cultural differences between Americans and Chinese when it comes to matrimony.

I'm 25, and most of my Chinese friends swear they wouldn't even ponder getting hitched much before 30 — and wouldn't wait much later, either.

The average age of a first marriage in the United States was 27.5 in 2006, when the US Census Bureau conducted the latest American Community Survey. Michigan, the state in which my wife and I were born and raised, hits this number right on the nose.

The curious thing about my local friends' reactions is that the average for China is 23.7, according to a 2007 Horizon Research Consulting Group survey.

Apparently, none of these pals, who are overwhelmingly middle-class urbanites — a demographic that tends to marry later — saw the survey. Most of them say the main reason they seek to tie the knot around 30 is financial stability. Before strolling down the aisle, they should own a house, and many also believe they ought to have a car.

But I do have one buddy who doesn't fit this mold. He's my age, and recently popped the question. He doesn't have a house and isn't even thinking of getting a car.

The two of us recently joined two older friends for a dinner at which our age and marriages became the main course of table talk. We were both grilled as to why we chose to marry so young and shot back shockingly opposite responses.

I married Carol because we rarely bicker, never get sick of each other no matter how much time we spend together, and when we're apart, we can't wait to be reunited.

I love her so much.

My friend is getting married because he and his girlfriend battle constantly, easily tire of one another and aren't always pining for the other's presence when they're apart.

He loves her so much.

Our tablemates congratulated me on my partnership and urged my friend to exercise caution in his.

No matter what culture you hail from, there are a lot of unwritten rules about how and whom one should marry.

For example, it's generally thought of as unwise in both the United States and China to wed at age 18. My parents did so 45 years ago and are happy together today.

Also, it's considered foolish to rush into marriage after only knowing each other for as little as three months. But that's exactly what Carol's parents did 26 years ago, and they are happy together today.

Another widely accepted no-no is getting married because you and your partner fight tooth and nail, need a lot of space from one another and aren't always missing each other when you're apart.

A lot of talk about relationships and wedlock I've engaged in with both foreign and Chinese friends in Beijing are anchored on cultural differences. The rest has focused on the similarities, especially the "should nots".

But individual personalities exercise more power than either inter- or intra-cultural norms when it comes to love — a pursuit in which rules are made to be broken, and sometimes breaking them is the only way to make sure hearts aren't.

I, for one, congratulate my soon-to-be-wed friend. His marriage might be an exception to the rule, and for that very reason, might be an exceptional marriage, one that's likely to last till death do them part.

ERIK NILSSON
(Nov 19, 2008)

51. Love's priceless, but weddings are expensive

The global economic crisis is forcing everyone to tighten their belts, but you can still cut loose on special occasions.

My wedding in May is one example of this. I wanted to hold a simple but stylish ceremony, but my mother immediately objected, saying that because I was the only child in the family, we had to make it special.

Recently, we visited a well-known wedding company in Hangzhou, Zhejiang province.

The manager suggested a traditional Chinese wedding, with an eight-bearer sedan chair to pick up the bride and a lion dance. Nice idea, but my apartment is some distance from the road, and I feared the unbearable summer heat would make the poor bearers faint along the way.

However, the enthusiastic manager was not easily deterred.

"You must do something special at the start of your wedding. How about using the Beijing Olympics?" he suggested.

As I struggled to figure out the connection between my wedding and the Games, the manager turned on his laptop and showed us his best work from last fall.

There was a video about the final countdown to the Olympics, featuring foot-shaped fireworks and drum performances, for instance. Finally, the scene cut to the restaurant in which the couple held their wedding.

"The custom-made video was on a big screen next to the stage. All the guests were excited about it. You like it, don't you?" he asked, cheerfully.

"Yes, I am very impressed," I replied, "but if we use it, my husband and I would be better off in sportswear than wedding gowns and suits."

The bride and groom's outfits are central to any wedding, and their prices vary enormously from 500 to 10,000 yuan ($74-1,471). The manager also recommended we include some music to entertain the guests, including violinists, Shaoxing opera singers (a traditional opera popular in southern China) and mask-changing performers. It was as if he were organizing a Spring Festival party rather than a wedding.

Each of the extra programs would cost at least 500 yuan, he said, and I'd also need to pay for their costumes and meals.

It is difficult to make such decisions on a limited budget. Noticing my concerned expression, the manager started to put even more pressure on me, saying I should not be reluctant to spend freely on my big day.

To emphasize his point, he showed us a video of a fabulous wedding that cost 280,000 yuan. The latest technology was used to set up a fireworks display that erupted when the bride and groom stepped into the hall. A model airplane carrying wedding rings flew to the stage during the vow exchange.

After watching it, I realized what I needed most was not money but rather a money-printer. On reflection, I decided to spend just 6,000 yuan on a master of ceremonies and a violinist.

I'd rather not spend all our savings on a wedding planner's grand visions.

XIE FANG
(Feb 26, 2009)

52. Putting love to the test

Before my engagement party started, we deposited some paraphernalia in our hotel room, number 801 — the number 8 being an auspicious numeral.

For two harrowing hours, I was left alone with my prospective mother-in-law.

Since I am only able to speak a few fragments of Mandarin, I was somewhat apprehensive at first. But it is amazing how far several words, coupled with several hand flourishes, can go.

For example, while getting dressed for the party, I asked my fiancé's mother whether I should wear socks or pantyhose. I pointed at my feet and asked *haishi* ("or"), then made a sweeping motion up my legs to signify pantyhose.

My dress was like something out of Piet Mondrian, with red, white and black stripes. I bought the dress in China expressly for this occasion because my dark velvet gown was considered too somber.

Then, the party exploded. We strode into the party room, which was decorated with the character for "double happiness" and showers of colorful balloons.

I greeted the army of relatives, foremost among them, the "back aunt". We gave her that nickname because she sets great store by good posture. She could win an Olympic gold in that discipline. For days, I had to perfect my posture, or *ting*.

When I greeted this particular aunt, the matriarch of the Zhu family, she

Chinese Calligraphy

Chinese calligraphy is very special Chinese art with a long tradition. The works displayed in the Calligraphy Gallery of the museum have exposed the evolution of Chinese characters, which shows people's long exploration in the beauty of the art of writing. So, we brief here some basic knowledge of Chinese calligraphy.

Oracle bone inscription — Characters inscribed on the turtle shells and animal bones of over three thousand years ago are the earliest systematic Chinese written language extant today, Most of them with a divinatory content were found at the Shang capital city, Yin (today's Xiaotuncun, Anyang, Henan). The development of the style from boldness to elaboration reflects people's attention on the art of writing.

Bronze inscription — Bronze inscriptions appeared in the Shang dynasty (ca. 16th-11th century BC) and fully developed in the Western Zhou dynasty (11th century-771 BC). The characters inscribed on the bronze wine vessel Bao You shown in the gallery displays the robustness of bronze inscriptions of early Western Zhou dynasty.

Qin simplified Seal script — The first emperor standardized the Chinese characters into one form-simplified Seal script after he united the whole country and started the Qin dynasty in 221 BC. The simplied Seal script with emphasis on the regularity and symmetry of each character, as exemplified by the work entitled Stone inscription of Tai Shan and the inscriptions on the standard weight measures, shows a very natural and plain style.

Official script — The Official script started to be adopted in Chinese writing in the late Warring States Period (3rd century BC and came into vogue in the Eastern Han dynasty (25-220). It moved the round linear turns of Chinese characters into square, thus initiating a new style of Chinese writing. The execution of heavy-down and light-up brushstrokes laid a good foundation for the later emergence of the Regular script.

Cursive script — In the Western Han dynasty, people developed a simpler form fo the Official script by linking together the lines of a character for quick writing, which is known as "Zhang's Cursive", the earliest form of the Cursive script. Later, it further broke free form the conventions of the Official script and brought into being the Cursive script with a distinctive aesthetic charm by links between lines as characters.

Two Wangs — The two famous Chinese calligraphers of the Eastern Jin dynasty-Wang Xizhi (321-379) and Wang Xianzhi (344-386), father and son, enjoyed a very high reputation in Chinese calligraphy history for their great contributions to the development of the Regular script, the Running script and the Cursive script, We have in our collection the Tang copies of their very famous works Shangyu Tie and Yatouwan Tie.

Tang Regular script — With a strict regulation and rigorous style, the Regular script attained its perfection in the Tang dynasty(618-907). A group of well-known calligraphers like Ouyang Xun, Yu Shinan, Zhu Suiliang and Xue Ji emerged in the early Tang period, and Yan Zhengqing and Liu Gongquan in the late Tang period. Among them, Yan Zhenqing's vigorous and dignified style represents the spirit of the Tang culture.

Four masters of the Song dynasty — Su Shi, Huang Tingjian, Mi Fu and Cai Xiang have been regarded as the four great calligraphers of the Song dynasty (960-1279). They all very excelled in the Running script with their individual styles.

Late Ming calligraphy — Some creative calligraphers of the late Ming and early Qing period (17th century) pursued more boldly and willfully the individuality in their calligraphy works to express their own artistic feelings and thoughts. The representative ones are Zhang Ruitu, Ni Yuanlu, Huang Daozhou, Wang Duo and Fu Shan.

Tablet inscription style of the Qing dynasty — Many calligraphers in the mid Qing period (18th century) advocated the calligraphic style of ancient tablet inscriptions and executed sedulously their own calligraphy works after the tablet inscription style. This kind of practice attained its peak in the late Qing period (19th century). The most important calligraphers of this style are Deng Shiru, Zhao Zhiqian and Wu Changshou. Their works, robust and natural, opened an new area or the continuous development of Chinese calligraphy.

Meaning	Oracle bone inscription	Bronze inscription	Simplified Seal script	Offcial script	Regular script	Runing script	Cursive script
Ox							
Moon							
Eye							
Vehicle							

1. Transcription of Ban Gu's essay in Regular script of Yan Zhenqing's style
by Dong Qichang (1555 -1636), Ming dynasty
The essay written by Ban Gu in the Eastern Han dynasty (25-220) gives praise to the ancient Chinese bronze food vessel Ding.

岳備貢兮江巘孫吐金莖兮敲浮雲寶鼎現兮色
氤氳煥其炳兮被龍文登祖廟兮享聖神貽靈德
彌億年　班孟堅寶鼎歌做顏魯公書　董其昌

2. Septasyllabic poem in Cursive script
by Zhang Bi (1425-1487), Ming dynasty
It is a sentimental poem written in eight lines and seven characters in each line.

3. Transcription of the tablet inscription of Huashan Temple in Official script
by Huang Yi(1744-1802), Qing dynasty
The tablet inscription is of the Han dynasty (205BC-AD220).

4. Calligraphy in Seal script
by Deng Yan (1743-1805), Qing dynasty
The writing is about ancient philosophy.

led me about the room, setting an excellent example by walking very straight. At one point, she even rubbed her back against a pillar in a cat-like manner. I tried to follow her lead and stalked around with *ting*. That broke the ice.

Next we were handed gifts — among them, surprise! — a red lacquer box with the omnipresent double-happiness symbol on it. There were also two Smurf-like Haibaos, totems of the Shanghai Expo.

Finally, it was time to eat. As usual, people started to appraise my chopstick skills, and I tried my best to stay cool and not let my lotus drop. During the meal, my fiancé and I had to pose for photos with every subdivision of his large family and give impromptu speeches.

I made a public confession of how much I still needed to learn about Chinese culture, such as when and where to deposit my shoes, and thanked everyone for warmly welcoming a *laowai* (foreigner).

While I was working away at the microphone, the meal continued. Chinese are very interested in the culinary arts and food is the focal point of life here and with good reason — it's delicious! In the background, strains of Elvis Presley, then the *Titanic* theme song.

I became more relaxed after I did a *ganbei* (toast) with "back aunt" and emptied my whole glass of wine. One little girl followed suit with her soymilk.

After our exchange of platinum rings and another impromptu speech, it was time to cut the pineapple cake, which prophesied: "100 years together and happy every day!" This was the first time I had seen people eat cake with chopsticks, and, believe me, it is possible and pleasant.

Upon leaving, each guest received not one, but — for luck's sake — two bars of Rittersport chocolate, slightly warped by the Shanghai heat. I had flown the chocolate in from Frankfurt.

TAMARA TREICHEL
(Sep 9, 2008)

53. A picture-perfect bride and groom

Things seem to run to a different schedule in China, they really do.

I'm sitting in a photographer's studio, while my Chinese fiancée, Ellen, is having her hair and make up done for our wedding photos.

You'll note that I say "fiancée", and not "wife" — we don't get hitched until May.

But we're having the photos taken now, because they'll look nice to show her relatives during the Spring Festival. I am assured this is a perfectly natural thing to do, and I shouldn't worry about anything.

Color me confused, but I don't think my parents did things this way. Their photos show them on the church steps, after they'd tied the knot, surrounded by family and friends.

Their pictures aren't a series of carefully choreographed fantasies played out like some elaborate romantic dream.

Or is that nightmare? Over the course of the morning, I'm dressed as an Austrian prince, a Chinese emperor, and, at one point, I pose with a cello.

And I don't think the Emperor suffered from a problem with choosing his wardrobe. A clap of his hands, and robes that fitted would have been immediately produced, tailored just for him.

I am built differently to the average Chinese groom. None of the pants will pull up my legs. There's only one shirt that fits me, and, even then, only if I stop breathing.

A frantic wardrobe assistant lets the seams out with a frenzy of scissors, pins and sighs.

I'm poked, prodded and manhandled into hundreds of different poses, none of which seem quite right to the photographer. My fiancée, on the other hand, just glides into the studio, stands in front of the background, and he

Li Min

snaps away quite happily.

I'm also told that I'll be retouched in Photoshop, which just fills me with delight. I always thought photographs were meant to be an accurate depiction of events, but it seems that just isn't romantic.

The other fun thing is that I am shorter than my fiancée. This doesn't bother me, but it is annoying the photographer no end.

A step is produced from some dark recess of the studio, and I have been teetering on it ever since. What's wrong with being short? I've been short all my life, and to start showing up as tall in photographs is definitely going to worry my parents: They're short, too!

Isn't it bad luck for the groom to see the bride in a wedding dress before the Big Day? If that's the case, I'm going to suffer pretty badly, as she's been in and out of half a dozen already.

I never knew these things came in colors other than white, but she's pretty much gone through the spectrum. I've been dressed to match some of them, most notably in a lilac suit — possibly recently used by the Mayor of Toytown.

Background rolls crash down behind me, and I keep falling out of ill-fitting shoes. Endless cups of hot water are pressed into my hand, as I'm led back and forth across the studio floor for what seems like days.

Despite all that, I'm remaining calm.

Tantrums could have been had, costumes flung, teeth gnashed and general chaos could have reigned supreme.

I console myself with this one, simple thought: After all this mucking around, all these changes and poses, the actual wedding should go smoothly … shouldn't it?

STUART BEATON

(Feb 9, 2010)

54. Marital bliss is free and invaluable

I recently attended the wedding of one of my best friends. The bride and groom, high-ranking 30-somethings in IT companies, dressed in elegant Western-style clothes. Guests who rushed to the French buffet all paused to have their photos taken by a wedding photographer.

The excited parents gave long speeches that roughly meant: "Finally, you are married, but hurry up with the baby."

It was all very romantic, just as I had dreamed of years ago. However, when I got married about 10 years ago, we didn't have the luxury of celebrating. We made the decision months before I received my Master's degree, and my husband had just worked for three years. In addition to being unaffordable, a banquet was also inconceivable for us, because both our families lived far away from Beijing.

We went to the civil affairs office where my husband's household registration was on file. A woman there said we needed a photo in addition to household registrations, ID cards and verification of our identity from his boss and my teacher.

To save time, we took a picture downstairs where there was only one photographer with one camera. My fiancé was clad in a worn-out blue shirt. Luckily, I had put on a coat with red and blue stripes, which was appropriate for the occasion.

That night, we called home to announce the news. Nobody seemed very excited, because we had been dating for four years and had visited both families to ask their approval.

But the next day, my Dad showed up. Well, actually, he was not there to surprise us but rather to attend a meeting. When he saw the photo, he smiled and said: "You look just like your Mum in our old wedding photo."

When they got married in the early 1960s, Mum was also a fresh graduate of a university in Northeast China, and Dad had been working in Shanghai for two years.

Before the 1970s, one's social class status could determine everything. My grandpa had organized porters to fight the Kuomintang in Sichuan province before 1949. His family was classified as "poor farmer".

When Mum told Grandpa her fiancé came from a "midlevel farmer" class family in Henan province, Grandpa wasn't happy. Fortunately, he found Dad to be an honest young man and finally agreed to his eldest daughter's choice.

Mum and Dad took their wedding photo in a small studio. They were lean, and their clothes were shabby and patched. But they had the most brilliant smile and shining eyes I've ever seen.

Recently, my cousin threw lavish wedding banquets in Shanghai, where she works in a foreign bank with her husband, and in Chongqing, where my aunt is a prominent middle school principal. They invited hundreds of relatives, friends and local celebrities to several restaurants.

Dad visited my cousin in Shanghai's prosperous Pudong New Area. He said she wouldn't stop complaining about her mother-in-law and how insufficient her 8,000-yuan ($1,107) monthly income is.

"She is too young to understand what life is," Dad said, sighing.

LIU JUN
(Jan 31, 2008)

4. CELEBRATE GOOD TIMES, C'MON!

55. The Boogiemen's bash on Fright Night

Halloween makes me grin like a jack-o-lantern.

It's such a sight when the little ghosts and goblins go on their annual parade. I'll always remember joining the hordes of trick-or-treaters who would march door-to-door, like miniature Avon salespeople, questing for tooth-rotting, taste bud-tantalizing sweets.

For months before the big night, my family would build elaborate haunted walks through the forest behind our house.

Gravestones were cast in cement and we built electric chairs from scrap wood. Come show time, we would ignite a pan of flash powder beneath the chair, while some condemned actor would scream and writhe while chewing blood tablets and spitting out their crimson contents like a sputtering lawn sprinkler.

The kids loved it.

We even built a guillotine, with a hole at the bottom into which someone would tuck his head. When the blade came whooshing down it would "chop off" a "head" created by stuffing a monster mask with newspaper. The disembodied noggin would whirl to the ground while the actor thrashed around.

When I got older I would hide behind our porch in a wolf mask and pounce out to scare the little beggars who came pounding on our door seeking sugary alms. I would be howling, with my fingers curled into claws.

It was so much fun.

None of this seemed too strange to me until I moved to China.

The Chinese take on Fright Night seems somewhat less grisly, with fewer guts but with all the glory. It's less Pagan and more party, and, consequently, many people here really dress to impress when they don their costumes.

However, since ready-made costumes are harder to find as the holiday is just gaining popularity, people are often more innovative with their outfits.

One girl we saw this year dressed as a giant fly. To create compound eyes, she used two mesh kitchen sieves, bending the handles to secure them to her head. She completed the outfit by connecting two large plastic wings, perhaps clipped off a children's costume, to her shirt.

I hit up a nightclub party with a panda, Supergirl, a baseball player, a witch, a Silk Market vendor and a ghost.

Since I hadn't found time to rent or make a costume, I appeared in a uniform I had gotten for a calisthenics performance. I don't think many people got it. I still don't, actually.

My wife wanted to go as a panda. But as she was unable to hunt down a black-and-white bear suit, she had to make due with smearing black eyeliner around her sockets and on the tip of her nose. Her costume washed off the next day in the shower.

One puzzled local looked at her ringed eyes and asked: "Are you the dead Harry Potter?" My equally confused wife didn't know what to say except for, "No".

Our friend, the ghost, was a huge hit and spent much of the night posing for pictures. It seems this is an ideal costume for China, as it is not only a big crowd pleaser but merely requires cutting holes in a sheet. He also wore sunglasses.

The Silk Market vendor got the idea while helping his brother cut deals at the shopping spot one day and tried on an employee's orange vest as a joke.

He was immediately rushed by a small army of real vendors who began bargaining with him to the amusement of a growing crowd. He went from bargaining in the vest to bargaining for the vest. He completed the getup with an ID badge and a large calculator.

His China-specific Halloween attire was convincing but not as convincing as one we saw at a big bash in Beijing's 798 art district last year.

When we asked a security guard at an unfamiliar party venue if he knew where the bathroom was in Chinese, he replied, "I don't work here", in English spoken with a perfect North American accent.

That made it immediately apparent he was from out of town and perhaps didn't even speak a lick of *putonghua*.

It was an embarrassing but honest mistake. That was a good costume.

ERIK NILSSON
(Nov 4, 2008)

56. Santa Clause is limping to town

There were about 60 drunken Santas rampaging down the street, with one catching piggyback rides on other St Nicks' backs.

The inebriated Kris Kringle imposter with the fractured ankle being lugged around on the shoulders of generous friends — that was me.

I had joined Beijing's SantaCon 2009 to shake myself out of winter hibernation. Like many living in the capital, I tend to burrow deep into the warm refuge of my apartment when polar winds blast the city.

Life was becoming as stale as last year's gingerbread cookies, and I thought SantaCon provided a good chance to do something different, to step out of my skin and into a St Nick suit.

As the event's website puts it: "SantaCon is a non-profit, non-political, non-religious and nonsensical annual Santa Claus convention, celebrating cheer, goodwill and fun. There's no particular reason to dress up in Santa suits, run around Beijing for hours, give gifts, sing songs, have strangers sit on our laps and decide who is naughty or nice. But it's a lot of fun, so Santa does it anyway."

Yes, I figured joining the mad march was a good way to go from ho-hum to "ho, ho, ho" fun for a day.

Two friends agreed, so we set off on that Saturday, a trio of slightly tipsy

St Nicks, one of whom was leaning on the others as he hopped down the street.

We grabbed a cab to the first stop, a pizza bar with exceptionally cheap booze generously poured out for the invading army of Father Christmases.

The cabbie acted like there was nothing odd about picking up three fumy foreigners clad in Christmas gear. But at least a few pedestrians who caught glimpses of us though the vehicle's windows did double takes. Some appeared puzzled and smiled. Others just looked puzzled.

Before long, there were several dozen Santas gulping down tipples, crooning Christmas carols and breaking into spontaneous bouts of dancing. My buddies insisted on carrying me along the rest of the route, with the next stop being Tian'anmen.

I remember thinking about how strange it was to be boozed up midday. Then I realized I was dressed like Santa. And so were several dozen other people. And I was being carried on their backs.

Considering the entire tableau, the part about drinking outside in the early afternoon didn't seem so weird anymore.

But because of my injury, our trio fell behind the rest of the holly, jolly march. And perhaps because of our intoxication, we boarded the subway heading in the wrong direction.

Eventually, I had to give up. My leg just hurt too darn much. And the copious tippling and baggy Santa suit were contributing to the preexisting difficulty of walking.

So I caught a cab home.

Because the St Nick outfit made locomotion cumbersome, I stripped it off immediately upon getting out the taxi — that is, aside from the pants.

These red trousers simply weren't going to come off unless I sat down to wrestle them from my bottom half — something that required sitting, which there was no place to do. But they weren't going to stay up, either, since the belt had torn apart. (Fortunately, I was wearing jeans underneath).

I was hobbling along when I encountered a neighbor, who asked something to the effect of, "What happened to you?"

She kindly offered to help. It was only then that I realized why she might be concerned.

There I was painfully limping around, half drunk, with red pants around my knees.

Having found the surreal adventure I'd sought, I stumbled through the door of my apartment.

I was thankful to return to my humdrum winter hibernation —— and very ready for a long winter's nap.

ERIK NILSSON
(Dec 31, 2009)

57. Good trip, no fall

It was a sheer drop to the bottom.

I was limping along the narrow mountain footpath with one arm wrapped around a disembodied length of sapling, the other around the shoulders of a local government type.

Wrapped in gauze around my fractured ankle were two egg whites and copious amounts of *baijiu* (Chinese liquor) mixed with a mysteriously pungent powder.

As I plodded along with the help of my crutches, it struck me this was a strange way to ring in the New Year, as I realized the date was Jan 1.

We were slogging toward Yunnan province's Zhukula village, a hamlet so remote that the main road into town is a rocky footpath about 5 km long but less than half a meter — sometimes about a dozen cm — wide, hugging the waist of a mountain range.

We were headed there to interview the inhabitants of this tiny settlement, which became home to China's oldest coffee forest when French missionaries took these magical beans there more than a century ago.

The remote village was still largely isolated from the outside world. No other foreigner had trod there since the missionaries. I was imaging what they were going to think when this goony American hopped into town, leaning on the trunk of a young tree one of our hosts had cut down with a sharp rock.

"Don't look down," the thoughtful official warned, as we crossed a particularly treacherous stretch of loose rocks above a declivitous drop.

I was glad I had stuffed the packing on my leg into my hiking boots, rather than wearing slippers as the doctor had advised.

The day before, the exceptionally gregarious Bingchuan county officials had insisted on taking me to a rural doctor. My ankle hadn't stopped stinging more than two weeks after I had injured it.

The accident was simply the result of me not noticing an upcoming curb

Li Min

while walking and fiddling with my mobile phone in the dark.

I'd figured it would heal quickly. But as the days turned into weeks, it seemed likely there might be more than a sprain causing the persistent need to hobble.

I was more than happy to just hop along for the rest of the trip — and my life — until nature took its course and whatever was wrong down there fixed itself. But my hosts were too kind to have it.

After discovering two small bone fractures in an X-ray and whipping up the potently acrid topical applicant, the supremely charitable doctor absolutely refused payment. I still have no clue why.

Perhaps it was the spirit of New Year's Eve. That mentality had at least overcome our hosts, who treated us to a jubilant night of gulping homemade liquor and crooning karaoke to videos projected on a canteen wall.

After midnight, the tipsy officials accompanied me to my room, where they heaped extra blankets on my body. One added fresh pours of *baijiu* to my gauze and massaged the foot, while the other two held my hands and offered affectionate words.

It was somewhat surreal but very endearing, and made for a New Year's Eve I'll never forget.

Another surprise came the next morning, when I was able to stand on the wounded foot with the other in the air for the first time in weeks.

By the end of the trip, I felt guilty for the thoughtfulness shown to me by the officials and my travel mates, Teacher Li and Xiao Guo. They cared more for my health than I do — and really showed it.

But, ultimately, it brought us closer and made the trip more interesting.

Sometimes, I've realized, a misstep or two can make the journey all the more memorable.

ERIK NILSSON

(Jan 13, 2010)

58. Go gently into the New Year

Most of my previous New Year's Eves were spent working at the copy desk back home in Calcutta, India, until a colleague came by and informed me another year had ended.

But 2009 was a special year. For the last 10 months I have been living in, and growing up with, Beijing — marveling at the grand scale and flawless handling of the CPPCC conferences held at the Great Hall of the People in March; walking along a spruced-up Chang'an Avenue in September to see the illuminations that defined and highlighted the historic buildings in the lead-up to the Republic's 60th anniversary celebrations in October; getting my anti-H1N1 jabs in November.

I wanted to see how Beijing rung out the old and embraced the new up close.

In Sanlitun, the courtyard of The Village looked strangely de-populated at 10:30 pm. A colleague who has seen a few years roll by in Beijing had told me this was the place to be — that they organized a countdown here with music and a free flow of drinks. I was enthused. I assumed Sanlitun was Beijing's answer to the celebrations on Times Square, Trafalgar Square or Sydney Harbor on New Year's Eve.

But the piazza looked more desolate than it would be on a regular evening. The stores announcing massive seasonal discounts were empty. The coffee shop, which would normally have its clientele spilling over outside its glass doors, was a picture of dereliction.

Behind the ice skating rink stood a small crowd, shivering in the cold as they brandished tickets, waiting to get to the basement. The guards, clad in heavy winter gear, stared at them, stoically, from the other side of the glass. So that's where the party was. On New Year's Eve, Beijingers into "serious" revelry chose to go underground. But it was already too saturated with people to admit any more.

I had heard there would be a fireworks display at Tian'anmen Square at the midnight hour. So that's where my colleague Yang Guang and I decided we would go. Once the cab touched down on Chang'an Avenue, it was

Li Min

skimming like a jet through the 12-lane passage, racing against itself.

Before he could drop us in front of the Great Hall of the People, a man jumped into the seat next to him.

"Ugh, it's so difficult to get any transport from here. What are you waiting for? Get in," he told his companion, impatiently, even as we were still seated inside the vehicle, trying to pay up.

We went up and the sidewalk a few times, expecting the fireworks to appear in the sky any moment and come down in a shower on the Monument to the People's Heroes.

At midnight the illumination on the Forbidden City gates went off. Yang Guang asked the guard standing nearby when the fireworks were due.

"Fireworks? What do you mean? There are no fireworks tonight." Apparently, there never are any on New Year's Eve.

We walked all the way to Wangfujing, past a bunch of diehard Westerners who insisted on leaping in the air, telling the world about the end of the noughties.

How we walked and waited, waited and walked around an incredibly un-peopled and frost-wrapped Wangfujing for what seemed like a millennium but in reality was just about an hour, is quite a tale. Eventually, a bus arrived to pick us up and drop us part of the distance.

Once seated in the heated interiors of the bus, I told Yang Guang I was happy Beijing did not meet my expectations. If it did not join the rest of the world's metropolises in unleashing a stream of revelers on the road, sometimes not even sure of what they were celebrating, it showed that Beijing preferred doing things its own way.

I am positive it has more surprises lined up for me in the coming year.

CHITRALEKHA BASU

(Jan 12, 2010)

59. Celebrating a festival without festivities

One promise I had made to myself while living in China was to find a real Chinese Spring Festival — that is, one in a village, with real people rather than foreigners and city types.

Having rented a farmhouse in just such a village, I didn't really have an excuse not to do so this year.

But memories of a night shivering there a few weeks earlier were still fresh, and having told my best friend how awful it had been, I was convinced — and hopeful — she would turn down the suggestion.

But she said yes.

"Didn't you HEAR what I told you about staying there? No bar? No heating? No shower?"

She was unmoved. Well, that was it; we had to go now. Socks and red wine in hand, and wrapped up 3-year-olds in tow, we jumped on a bus.

After lighting the fire under the *kang* (the brick bed we would all be sleeping on was the only source of heating in the house), we roamed the village to look for the Spring Festival.

It was spooky. There was no sign of anyone. Suddenly, there was a burst of crackers and some smoke. We rushed over but all we saw was a pile of black, smoking tubes.

All the houses in the village look inward, facing the yards around which they are built, with no windows looking out and just a front door to gain access. All the doors were tightly shut. Presumably families were huddled up inside, wrapping their dumplings, adding fuel to their *kang* and now and then letting off a few firecrackers.

In a strange way it felt cozy to be outside in the freezing cold, imagining the warmth within.

But this was New Year's Eve, and we had thought the village would celebrate collectively. We were looking for dragon dancing, fireworks, singing.

We gave up looking for Spring Festival celebrations, hunkered down in my *kang* room, found food of sorts, told stories and felt pretty snug ourselves.

At 5 to midnight, with two children sleeping and a third bottle of wine opened, we struggled onto the roof. I found myself feeling even more respect for my friend, who, sober and in daylight, hates climbing that rickety old ladder.

Suddenly, from the blackness of the valley way below came simultaneous showers of sparks and towers of fire flowers stretching hundreds of yards, fountain after fountain. And behind, the village suddenly came alive, with blast after blast and the loudest fireworks I've ever heard, just a few meters away.

For half an hour we watched this spectacular show — and, miraculously, didn't fall off the roof.

Maybe it was the wine. Maybe it was the snuggling together on the *kang*. Perhaps it was burning half my landlord's entire winter stock of timber or even having another adult to share with. But we all slept like the logs I'd seen go up in smoke and in the morning were still toasty. We even went for a walk.

Who would have thought it had happened. It was as if the midnight minutes on the roof had been a dream. There was no outward sign that the most important date of the year had just passed, with the beauty of the hills undisturbed, the crows cawing and the morning light, golden and still.

I felt very calm, stepping off the bus in Beijing. Until, that is, a crackle right under my feet sent me scurrying on a pavement completely covered with red paper and lined with people clutching incense as they lined up to enter the Lama Temple.

Noise! Litter! People! Fireworks in the middle of the street!

Aha, Spring Festival. I had found it, at last.

DEBBIE MASON

(Feb 18, 2008)

60. Love wrapped up in dumpling dough

I know two things that I'll be asked to do every year to amuse my wife Ellen's family during Spring Festival.

One is lighting the fireworks. The other is making *jiaozi*, or dumplings.

Fireworks I have no problems with. Pyrotechnics I can bend to my will, and make them perform as they should.

Dumplings, however, are another story.

When I think of dumplings, I envision little balls floating on top of a rich, hearty stew. Sometimes, I conjure up the image of dumplings in a sweet syrup. Even potato gnocchi in a creamy sauce comes to mind.

Chinese dumplings don't fit into those categories, with their payload of filling in a thin dough casing.

They shouldn't be such a hard task. I've made ravioli before, and that's the same idea except that ravioli is made with a form or mold and is not judged by eye.

That's where I seem to go wrong.

I can make the filling for dumplings, that's not a problem. Chopping and mincing the meat, prawns and vegetables, stirring them together — all of that I can handle.

Even the dough for the wrappers is straightforward. It's not as tricky as brioche or even bread dough. I just can't form them.

Luo Jie

Ellen's family gathers around the table to watch my struggles. On occasion, they've invited their friends, just to make sure no one's missing out on what must surely be the show of the year.

First, I roll the dough into long strips, and pinch off the right amount for a wrapper. I take the little lump of dough, form it into a circle with the rolling pin, place it in the palm of my hand, and the theatrics begin.

With the wrapper in my left hand, I take a pair of chopsticks in my right and try to gauge just how big of a lump of filling I need. I drop the filling into the wrapper and start to try and fold it.

While I'm pinching along the edge of the dumpling, the filling is being forced away from the seam. The more I work it, the thinner one end is, while the other end bulges. The dumpling looks like a ball with a fringe of dough on the outside. Of course, if I put too little filling in the wrapper, I end up with a sausage-shaped dumpling that's all dough.

All the while, I can feel several sets of eyes glued to my every move. I swear I can hear the faint start of a giggle. Sweat forms on my brow, as my concentration is so fierce.

Neither of my two dumplings comes even close to the perfect form of their companions. While I am struggling with the two, everyone else has made about a dozen or so each, and I'm starting to feel like I've missed out on some really big secret somewhere along the line.

There must be classified dumpling schools across China, where pupils are given extensive coaching in how to fold the perfect dumpling, with exactly the right amount of filling in it. The graduates of these schools are forbidden to share their knowledge with foreigners, on pain of having their folding fingers twisted like dough!

Why do I think that? Because every time I ask for help, I'm told that I'm doing OK. But I know I'm not!

I've resorted to watching cooking shows, browsing recipe sites and even practicing with Play-Doh.

This year, I thought I'd finally broken the curse of the funny shaped dumpling, but it didn't matter. I discovered that despite what my dumplings look like, I'm part of my wife's family — forever.

And that's the most important thing that I've learned about Chinese dumplings: They bring people together, no matter what.

STUART BEATON

(Feb 23, 2010)

61. Dumplings stuffed with memories

On the lunar New Year's Eve, I sent my friends an SMS: "Homemade *jiaozi* are the most delicious, may everyone have a round tummy."

I was visualizing the dumplings of minced pork, fragrant mushrooms, baby cabbage, Chinese water chestnuts, leeks and fresh eggs.

While not the best-written New Year's wish of the zillions flying across the globe among Chinese speakers, it was a sincere hope from a happy family.

Many foreigners find *jiaozi* delicious to eat but formidable to make. Stuart Beaton, a great chef and English teacher based in Tianjin, wrote about how he sweats while making *jiaozi* in front of his Chinese fiancée's family.

For me, and most Chinese, the essence of making *jiaozi* is not about feeding the *chanchong* — a stomach worm fond of good food. Rather it's about enjoying the camaraderie shared by "long-time-no-see" family members, as everyone pitches in to make the year's most important meal.

Even those who know nothing about cooking get in on the act. My son, almost 5, beamed with joy and pride as he sat on a stool, cleaning the leeks. This was his second attempt at making *jiaozi*.

I put some filling on the wrapper, and he tried to fold it without squeezing out too much filling. We joked that a steamroller had squashed his works, which made him grin wider.

He has become a fan of *Transformers* and has named himself "Iron Hide" and me "Optimus Prime". For some reason, his father is "Road Roller".

As a mother, I'm often upset to see youngsters' apathy toward Chinese values. This year, I found that making *jiaozi* offered a great opportunity to share with them the essence of Chinese culture — the importance of family, tradition and love.

Archaeologists say the oldest *jiaozi*, unearthed from the tomb of a duke in Shandong province, are more than 2,500 years old.

Li Feng

There are numerous legends about the delicacy to share at family gatherings, but my favorites always come from my childhood.

In the 1970s, food was scarce and making *jiaozi* was a big annual event. We used Dad's huge, specially made pinewood board, logged from the mountains, to make *jiaozi*, noodles, buns and pastries.

My older sister and I delighted in baking thumb-sized dough balls in the woodstove and were enthralled by the many kinds of dumplings Dad made. In addition to the ordinary, chubby, crescent-shaped varieties, he also made little mouse-shaped dumplings with wheatear patterns.

"Your grandma could roll a wrapper with one hand and wrap a *jiaozi* with the other," Dad would say, as a perfectly round wrapper took shape under his rolling pin.

Mum always fussed over the perfect match of wrappers and fillings. If there were more wrappers, Dad would make small pancakes using two of them. And if there was more filling, Dad would hurry to make more dough.

Because of her limited *jiaozi*-making skills, Mom always boiled them. When the water had boiled three times and the dumplings had all puffed up and floated like plump white ducklings, Dad would carry a big bowl of steaming dumplings to the table. We sisters would set the table with bowls of soy sauce, vinegar and garlic.

San Mao, a popular Taiwan writer in the 1980s, once entertained her Spanish husband's boss with *jiaozi*. She put a vase of bird-of-paradise flowers on a beautiful tablecloth and laid out the "crane-like" dumplings. It was quite charming.

One day, if my son goes abroad and meets new friends, I hope he will not only enchant them with tales of *Transformers* but also with those of delicious *jiaozi*.

LIU JUN
(Feb 24, 2010)

62. Having a blast during Spring Festival

The first time a rocket hit me, I threw my hands over my face, thinking I should be in pain but feeling none. As I lowered my hands, a smile spread across my face because the firework meant this year wouldn't be like the last.

Last year, I had learned the hard way that the most important Chinese festival, Chunjie, is all about real estate. It's location, location, location.

For my first Spring Festival, I was in the wrong location. That night, I wandered lonely streets in eerie silence in Tianhe, Guangzhou's ultra-modern district.

The problem with Tianhe is that Chunjie is a time for Chinese to return to their ancestral hometowns. No one's ancestral home is located in an ultra-modern district of high-rises that was rice fields only 20 years ago.

To be fair, there was the thrill of discovery: That night I finally discovered what Tianhe's sidewalks really looked like, since this was the first time I had ever seen them any less crowded than a rugby scrum.

But the joy of discovery wasn't enough to quiet my rumbling stomach as I walked past all my favorite restaurants — all shuttered. Handwritten signs hung on the shutters: "Closed for Chunjie."

So I went to bed, hungry and alone in a now-empty city of millions, in an apartment without heat, in confusion about what the big deal was with Chunjie.

But this year, I was in Longyan, Fujian province, where the airspace was so packed that an errant rocket from the arsenal of a pack of young whippersnappers on the side of the road found its way to my face. When it hit me, I was so elated that I had finally found where the Chunjie action was that I watched the lights swirling in my vision and counted them as my lucky stars.

Soon the stars I was seeing weren't just in my eyes. They were sprouting and blooming in mere fractions of seconds amid the cracks and ravines of

Li Min

the streets of Longyan. And as I watched from the 15th-floor hotel room, far above the other buildings in town, I realized these stars blew the 4th of July out of the water.

The explosions were so loud I couldn't hear the TV blaring a few meters away with the New Year extravaganza, the CCTV Spring Festival Gala. Fireballs erupted so close to the building that I could have reached out and touched the beautiful fire trails.

When I ventured out onto the streets that night, my stomach was full. The fireworks' shredded paper casings fell from the sky onto my face as I gazed up in awe. While I was out, the rich sulfur smoke settled over the city and into my room, filling it with an acrid smell.

As a foreigner in China, it's easy to feel welcomed but hard to feel part of the culture. Intense language study doesn't remove all the barriers. I learned as much when I sat that evening staring blankly as the jokes of the annual CCTV comic "cross-talk" performance sailed over my head faster than the fireworks outside.

But the pounding explosions and colorful sparks in the sky outside knew no language or culture.

My head was foggy with a sulfur-induced hangover when I awoke the next morning. Outside, I saw the sidewalks for a second time like I had never seen them before. Overnight, they had sprouted a covering of red casings, as if a million pounds of red confetti had been airdropped on the city.

Tradition says that fireworks are supposed to scare away evil spirits from sticking around for the New Year. White-skinned foreigners have been called *yang guizi*, "ghosts", in China for as long as anyone can remember. But the rocket that pegged me in the face that day convinced me that this tradition was something worth sticking around for.

THOMAS TALHELM
(Feb 11, 2010)

63. Swept up in family matters

The cold wind blew clouds of ashes around the mounds, and we shivered and drew our coats closer.

It was Qingming Festival, the Tomb Sweeping Day, and I'd been invited to go with my wife Ellen's family to help tend to her family's graves. It wasn't the sort of offer I'd had before, so I was keen to take the opportunity to go to the countryside, to see what life was like outside of suburban Tianjin.

The day started early — very early. I was prodded awake at 6 o'clock, a time I don't often see, and gently herded downstairs and into Ellen's father's car. I dozed off and on in the back seat, as he drove for almost 90 minutes outside of the city. About halfway along, we stopped to buy apples and Chinese white liquor (*baijiu*) at a small roadside stall.

As the larger sealed roads gave way to small dirt tracks, I began to notice conical mounds in the fields, topped with a large rock or clod of dirt. I didn't pay them much mind, thinking those were probably well markers or something agricultural in nature.

Eventually, we stopped at a field that seemed to have an awful lot of these mounds on it. It was then that it dawned on me that they were burial sites and the reason why we were there.

In an extremely surreal moment, I was handed a shovel by Ellen's father.

Terrible horror movie clichés spun through my head, and I had a sudden vision of having to reprise the work of Burke and Hare. I was relieved when Ellen told me it was to chip the weeds off the mounds and nothing nastier!

Ellen's mother set out in the lead, looking for her ancestors' tombs. After a few wrong turns, and a bit of back tracking, we found them and set to work

Li Min

clearing away the weeds and rubbish that had gathered on their sides. It was my job to skim the surface of the mound with the shovel and smooth it off.

After we'd made the graves neat and tidy, I helped Ellen's father start a small fire, into which Ellen's family added sheets of paper with holes punched in them. I asked Ellen what they were doing. She told me they were sheets of coins and that by burning them they were sending them to their ancestors to make their afterlives more comfortable.

At nearby mounds, other families were burning more elaborate paper objects. I saw model cars and a boat go up in flames — even a small mahjong set.

As the offerings we had brought burned, Ellen's mother talked slowly and carefully to the mounds.

"What's she saying, Ellen?"

"She's telling her parents all about you — what a good man you are, how we're getting married, everything."

"I hope she's telling them only the good things ..."

We lit a bundle of incense sticks and carefully placed them before the grave. We placed the apples next to them, and Ellen's father poured the *baijiu* over the mound.

Finally, I laid out a string of firecrackers and lit them. As they burst and popped, we bowed three times to Ellen's ancestors. The wind swirled the red paper around my ankles and carried it off across the fields surrounding us.

I shouldered the shovel and took Ellen's hand for the walk back to the car, happy in the feeling that I was now a part of a family tradition — that I was becoming more and more a part of my new Chinese family and of their lives.

STUART BEATON
(April 13, 2010)

64. Remembering people and traditions lost

The first I'd ever heard of the Qingming Festival was when I was told my friend was going home for the Tomb Sweeping Festival.

A translator friend said Qingming meant "pure brightness" and traditionally also heralded the beginning of springtime planting around April 5. I was in Hong Kong during that time, and the hillside cemeteries looked like hundreds of campfires were burning. I was alarmed until a friend informed me that people were just burning up the sweepings from the gravesites and then igniting paper offerings and joss sticks.

I was driving through the countryside on my way to a day of hiking outside Hangzhou during Qingming when I found the hillsides lively with people coming and going, carrying flowers and brooms. Suddenly I was struck by the similarity to a much-anticipated day in my childhood, Memorial Day. This American national holiday began after the Civil War to honor the deceased soldiers and is now held on the last Monday in May.

Living in a very small mountain community, we children were eager for any excitement. On Memorial Day we brought flowers from our yards, usually lilacs since little else was blooming yet in that northern clime. Lessons were suspended so that we could join the veterans of our town. The children and most townsfolk walked solemnly to the small stone etched with the names of our servicemen who had died. Many families had someone memorialized there.

A trumpeter played the mournful song, *Taps*. A veteran laid a wreath on the stone, and we all held our hands over our hearts. Then we walked the mile or so to the town cemetery.

Someone shot a rifle for the traditional 21-gun salute given to fallen soldiers. Candles were lit at every one of their graves.

Liu Yanfeng

Watching the adults carefully, we children were impatient for the solemn part to be over. We were supposed to help clean the graves of the whole cemetery. Instead, we usually tossed our lilacs in a heap and started chasing each other around the gravestones. We'd be pulled back by our teachers and families and encouraged to pray for the deceased.

Then came the good part — picnics. What's a special day without special food?

When I see how much it means to the Chinese people to have this day to honor their ancestors, I wish I'd been a bit more reverent as a child. When I was raising my children, we lived far from where my family was buried, so I fear I didn't raise them with any real sense of feeling connected to our departed relatives. We lived in a much bigger town, so while their school did honor Memorial Day, it was by watching a parade. Viewing is so different from feeling part of something as I did as a child.

I envy the Chinese families I see who come together as several generations follow hallowed rituals. It may be that the younger members are more interested in running around, as we were, but they will look back at these occasions with great fondness as they, someday, bring their little ones to the sites of their ancestral history. Modern life can be so confusing and changes so fast that a family who pauses once a year to honor those who have gone on before gives a message of continuity.

I think it says: "We were, we are and we will be family. On this spot you, too, may rest someday surrounded by loved ones. You will always be cared for here."

I didn't give that to my children because we were so far away from our hometown, chasing the American Dream of prosperity. As more Chinese travel far to chase the Chinese Dream of prosperity and are unable to join their families at Qingming, will some of them someday feel the regret that I feel?

SANDRA LEE
(April 2, 2009)

5. MEETING THE REAL CHINESE

65. Learning life's lessons

My name-card collection bursts out of several boxes and runs the gamut of professions and personalities.

This is thanks to the Chinese custom of exchanging cards with nearly everyone you meet, no matter how fleetingly.

But the card I cherish most was given to me by Yang Zhouxing. It came into my possession while I was speaking to a class of middle school students in rural Sichuan province's Pingwu county, a quake-affected area where the youngsters, who studied in makeshift classrooms, had never glimpsed a foreign face.

The May 12, 2008 quake destroyed classrooms in nearly all of Pingwu's 146 schools, killing 344 students and 13 teachers. In total, 31,079 pupils and 2,631 instructors were affected in the county, according to Pingwu's education bureau.

Many of the children at the middle school we visited lost family, friends and their homes.

But their spirit of hope had not only survived but also shined brightly, and did so in a surprising and inspiring way.

They talked of dreams — to become doctors, translators, singers, world travelers.

In an in-class activity we did with the students, the overwhelming majority wrote that they believed they would realize their ambitions through persistence.

Senior level 2 student Xue Chen summed up the students' ethos: "We must keep moving and never give up!"

Shortly after I gave my first talk on cross-cultural exchange, I was stormed by swarms of students who practically climbed over one another to thrust their notebooks toward me, asking for my autograph.

I'd become accustomed to the extra attention foreigners receive outside of metropolitan or tourist areas — or so I'd thought. Being asked to scrawl my John Hancock across notebooks and textbooks — that was a new one for me.

Luo Jie

One of the kids asked for my phone number, address, e-mail, MSN and QQ.

I retrieved my name-cards from my wallet and slipped one into his hand.

This detonated an explosion of fingers, and, in seconds, the students had confiscated the entire stack. They stared at these prizes with wide-eyed grins, as if the cards were winning lottery tickets.

I smiled, too.

The bell clanged, heralding the end of class, and students stampeded from the makeshift buildings.

As the kids funneled out of the structure where I had been speaking, the boy to whom I'd handed the first card approached me and sheepishly announced he had something he wanted to give me.

He had carefully printed his name, Yang, mobile number and QQ in blue ink on a rectangular scrap of cardboard.

Yang presented me the card with both hands.

"This is my card," he said, flashing a toothy grin that dipped when he bowed slightly while hoisting the gift toward me.

Yang and his classmates had been astonished at seeing a foreign face. I am still awestruck at seeing their perseverance of spirit in their hearts.

I have no doubt they all can realize their dreams. They've already shown their abilities to surmount challenges and demonstrated the can-do attitudes that are crucial to success and happiness.

On days when I feel discouraged and frustrated and I catch sight of Yang's card on my desk, my thoughts drift back to him and his classmates.

And I remember the lesson they've taught me — to keep moving and never give up.

ERIK NILSSON
(Nov 11, 2008)

66. The godfather's not Marlin Brando

It all happened so fast.

There was a toast, a speech and gift giving, followed by the ceremonial offering, and lighting, of a cigarette.

Before anyone could say "*gandie*", I had a Chinese godfather.

The crowd watching the impromptu ceremony in the banquet hall went nuts with hoots and applause, as the new family members guzzled goblets of *baijiu* and hugged onstage.

But what did it all mean?

Actually, this particular event, while rare and perplexing, was a manifestation of relationship norms in China that highlight how different they can be from those in the West.

I had met my *gandie*, who insisted I call him *zhongguode baba* (Chinese father) until I learned the term for godfather, on a media trip.

Before we became apparent family, I had called him Mr Zhang. I didn't even know his given name. Someone later translated it from his business card. Zhang is general director of the Hunan provincial information office's media center and was leading a delegation of reporters on a trip through Hubei and Hunan provinces.

I'd thought of him as an official — and as a pretty darn nice guy — until just before that moment.

Now, we were mashed into each other's sweaty bosoms and apparently related. He turned to the crowd and announced he was now responsible for the young American's life. He gave his top-of-the-line watch, which he says he's had for 10 years, as a symbol of this powerful bond.

These grand gestures aroused a nearly equal sense of joy and bafflement. Why was he doing this?

The reason he gave the crowd: "I really like him." But many people like one another and never opt to cultivate surrogate family ties.

He stressed this was a serious relationship that extended far beyond friendship. And he proved it the next day when travel arrangements back to Beijing from Hunan hit a snag. He got on the phone and, through a lot of finagling, arranged for drivers, a hotel and a train ticket.

Along the way, Zhang made sure there were meetings with my *ganma* (godmother) and little brother — also of no blood relation to Zhang.

But after returning to Beijing, the five Ws about this relationship remained as befuddling as ever.

It seems this is merely an extreme example of what can epitomize the real relationships in China, especially those between foreigners and locals.

Compared to associations solely among Westerners —

Luo Jie

strongly influenced by individualism and similar cultural identities — those shared by Chinese and foreigners are often characterized by a deeper level of commitment based on a shallower level of familiarity. The people in these relationships might know less about — but certainly are more committed to — one another, compared to most foreigner-to-foreigner, especially Westerner-to-Westerner, ties.

Many foreigners here are more willing to make greater sacrifices in terms of money, time and convenience for their Chinese pals than for foreign friends whom they might be more intimate with. That's because these Chinese friends would do the same for them — and nearly always do, usually on a sweeping scale scarcely imaginable among at least Westerners.

And as the relationship deepens, so does this commitment.

In addition to the fact that we've known each other for only a short time, Mr Zhang doesn't speak any English and I speak Chinese like a small child.

But as our communication abilities improve and time brings us closer together, the depth of our commitment to the relationship will grow, too.

And because of the way made-in-China relationships work, I'm eagerly awaiting that.

ERIK NILSSON
(May 27, 2009)

67. Singing the Super Girl's praises

My fiancé's mother has been enamored by Super Girl Li Yuchun (Chris Lee) since I first met her in 2006.

I bought her a birthday gift in Beijing and tucked it away in my suitcase. When we got to Shanghai, my prospective mother-in-law was eager to wash our laundry.

To my surprise, she had already unpacked the suitcase, found the Super Girl CD and looked at me with an expression, as if pleading: "*Wo de*? (Mine?)." She reminded me of an excited girl who had just discovered a gift under the Christmas tree.

Upon my second visit to Shanghai, her adoration for Li had not abated. If anything, it had grown more ardent.

For example, the dining table had a glass pane covering not only the plaid tablecloth but also calendar pages of Li, rocking away in a blouse shaped like a trumpet lily and with windswept hair, as if she had just stepped off a ship. Yes, Li was everywhere in her house, and when we bit into our wontons, there she was, watching our every move.

During one of the lunchtime conversations with my fiancé's mother, I asked her about Li. Her eyes glowed as she told me that the singer originally came from Sichuan province but had gone to Beijing to work.

Once, my fiancé's mother invited us to watch a recording of a Li Yuchun concert she had attended. There was Li, singing in her husky voice and gyrating in her iconoclastic costumes — a red matador outfit, a fuchsia-colored Peking Opera costume and then a glittering sports getup. I noticed that most of Li's fans were middle-aged women, wielding fluorescent sticks and hailing her with enthusiastic shouts of "*Wo ai ni!*" (I love you!).

While listening to Li's music, my prospective mother-in-law would sometimes sing along in a sweet treble that contrasted well with Li's alto. In a gesture of filial piety, my fiancé downloaded several of Li's songs for his mother's iPod so she could listen to her idol while commuting to work.

I also noticed that her short hair cut resembled Li's, and its reddish hue was not unlike Li's tawny brown. Even her manner of dressing was a hidden homage to Li — sportive, yet undeniably chic.

My fiancé's other relatives scoff at his mother's undiminished enthusiasm for the Super Girl. Obviously, they do not find Li's unfeminine style aesthetically pleasing. Yet I share my prospective mother-in-law's admiration. This Super Girl has something generous about her, a warm aura that embraces everything she does.

When I asked my fiancé's mother why she adored Li, she replied that she was impressed by the singer's original style and purity. There is nothing fake about this young woman. Perhaps to her, Li also represents the missed opportunities of youth and a possibility to live them out through this shooting star.

Indeed, I was surprised to learn that Li is not only another pretty face on postage stamps or a poster girl for toothpaste ads but also is actively involved in charity. For example, she helps people living with HIV/AIDS and poor children with leukemia by auctioning off her old costumes or donating the proceeds of a concert. Now, isn't that a Super Girl?

Luo Jie

TAMARA TREICHEL
(Nov 5, 2008)

68. Look behind to find kind folks

A few nights ago, a friend and I rode in a crowded elevator to have dinner together. When the door opened on the top floor, my friend instinctively stepped out first, brushing past a middle-aged Caucasian woman on the way.

There was a brief pause, and the woman sneered: "Polite."

I hesitated for a beat. Should I tell her to wipe off her sarcastic superiority, and take it or leave it? This is what China is like. People don't necessarily follow Western norms of decorum. But deep down, people like my friend, who is ignorant of proper elevator-exit etiquette, are nice — in a very Chinese way.

Then, I realized that five years ago, when I first moved back to China, I would probably have mouthed a condescending "polite" as well. Back then, after a 12-year absence, I was both repulsed and fascinated by people spitting in the streets, shoving at bus stops and talking loudly in public. I was like a foreigner in my own country.

On a month-long trip along the ancient Silk Road from Xi'an to Kashgar, I met Old Wang in the sleeper car to Urumqi. When he found out I was traveling by myself, he asked if I'd like to join his group for a backpacking trip to Yili. "Hell yeah!" I said.

In Urumqi, Old Wang found me a military backpack and a sleeping bag.

He stuffed the tent and the cans of food in his own backpack.

"You should carry a lighter load," he said.

I had never backpacked before.

Old Wang was in his early 50s, I think. The Xinjiang government bureaucrat had a chubby face and a bald head. With his daughter heading off to university and his wife a busy doctor, Old Wang had taken to backpacking in the Xinjiang wilderness with a group of friends.

He had typical Chinese manners — spitting on the sidewalk and arguing loquaciously for pennies in the grocery market. Yet, from the moment we met, he treated me like a son.

When the hired coach reached Lake Sailimu after an 18-hour bumpy ride, my upset stomach turned into a nastier lower bowel movement. So from the moment we started the hike, he was constantly by my side. "How's your stomach?" he would ask. "Should we take a little break?"

During stops for meals, he would light the gas stove and cook instant noodles while I rushed behind the bushes. Then he would carry the noodles to me, a diarrhea pill right next to the paper bowl. When we reached the campground, he set up the tent all by himself. After dinner, as the sun set and the stars rushed out of the blue velvet of a sky, I'd sit with the group and watch them playing cards, guffawing and joking under the camp light.

We returned to Urumqi after five days. On the last day in the city, Old Wang accompanied me to do some shopping. He was quiet most of the time.

At the end of the day, he asked me to visit him again, in his uncouth, loud and endearing way.

During the past five years, I have grown used to the littering and the chaos in the cities. I have become desensitized to the quarrels in the street, and the pushing and the shoving.

Sometimes, the city and the people still get on my nerves. But I have learned to breathe in deeply whenever that happens and remind myself that

beneath the uncivil surface, some — or many — of the people in the street are capable of genuine kindness like Old Wang, which is much more important than behaving "properly".

Spitting, of course, is different. It's just not sanitary.

XIAO HAO

(July 9, 2009)

69. A good buddy gone, in a puff of smoke

There was a humble cigarette stand in the community where I live. Its shabby cover could barely ward off wind or rain, but the cigarettes were the best in the neighborhood, with many varieties on offer at reasonable prices.

I often visited the stand, because its owner was a kind, honest youngster from Anhui province. The 17-year-old lived all by himself in this huge city. Every morning before 7, the young man would sit behind his cigarettes in a worn-out green cotton overcoat. With hair uncombed and nose running, he greeted acquaintances with a hearty smile.

He was known in the neighborhood as Lao'er — a fond title for the family's second child. Lao'er was quiet, but when he spoke, he was outspoken. Whenever I bought a pack and took out a cigarette but couldn't find my lighter in any of my pockets, Lao'er would hand me one, grinning broadly and saying: "Big bro, this is for you."

I sometimes stopped by his stand at mealtime. A bowl of the cheapest noodles without any meat from the nearby restaurant was his usual meal. He always raised the bowl to my face. As the steam blurred my view, he would say: "Big bro, have you eaten? Have some if you haven't."

Occasionally, Lao'er surprised me.

Once I was carrying out my wife's orders to greet her bosom friend. I bought a pack from Lao'er before we headed home.

Lao'er took one look at the charming lady beside me, and then whispered conspiratorially: "Big bro, your wife returned home half an hour ago. Don't take her home. There's a warehouse behind my stand. Well, just in case you need a place…"

I laughed so hard that I couldn't light my cigarette or find enough words to clear the young man's suspicions.

A few days ago, when I got up and found no cigarettes at hand, I hurried out, only to discover broken tiles and pebbles in place of the crowded grocery stores, photo studios and food stands. They were gone overnight.

I asked the security guard what had happened. He merely gestured at a nearby board that read: "All the flat houses in the community have been removed for a better environment."

Did the guard know where Lao'er had gone? No.

That good-natured young fellow who had greeted me almost daily for more than a year had simply vanished into thin air. Who knows when and in what unexpected corner I will bump into that Lao'er who generously offered me noodles and a warehouse.

I then remembered many other such nobodies in this enormous city.

Back in college, there used to be a dumpling stand. The young man who cooked for us everyday was also called Lao'er. The Henan province native also disappeared overnight when illegally constructed buildings were torn down.

As I prepared my doctoral thesis, I often bought used books from a young man of Shandong province. When the *hutong* alley gave way for high-rise buildings, he, too, was gone.

Even though these men humbly called Lao'er disappear from our lives every day, the diligent folks from outside Beijing create the liveliest part of our urban scene.

HU XUDONG
(Feb 14, 2007)

70. Xi Shi is a cut above

In the market close to my home, my wife and I have found some honest providers for our daily lives. For tropical fruits, we go to a couple from Inner Mongolia. For rice, we visit an auntie from Shanxi. For tea, we hit up the store of Miss Flower. For carp and catfish, it's a "fish professor" who wears bookish spectacles.

As for meat, we pay homage only to "Xi Shi at the Chopping Board".

Xi Shi is one of four leading ancient beauties who lived some 2,500 years ago. My first encounter with her modern version was a shock.

In the hall where more than 100 meat men gather, I often feel like I have gone back in time, as if I have been dropped into a bustling agricultural society.

One butcher has just beaten up a naughty son-in-law. His neighbor has sold out of meat and only has bones left. While one woman glares at a picky customer with the vicious looks of a character from *Outlaws of the Marsh*, a stout man nearby has just put down the knife and is reclining like a monk.

Amid the shouts and chopping, through flashing knives under the red lamps, I suddenly caught sight of a lady. Her face was as bright as a peaceful moon hanging over the river at midnight. Her voice was that of the melodious and charming babbler exercising on the bamboo early in the morning.

Wearing an apron, she was slicing the spareribs with a cleaver, but doing so in a clean and elegant way resembling the locomotion of a ballerina.

Deeply struck by her beauty, I rushed over and carried away a pile of pork that we couldn't possibly finish in a week and established a rapport with her. She came from Nanchong, which neighbors my hometown in Sichuan province. When beauty is mixed with delicacy and nostalgia, I consider it the greatest fortune of my life.

I have a belief: Sichuan and Chongqing produce the country's best pork. I can hardly buy meat from dealers of other areas. An ideal chunk of pork must be shaped in the dialect of the home to spicy food.

One must share the pleasant findings with one's better half. My wife, who always discounts my accounts of beauty, came back from the market acknowledging my discovery.

In fact, it seems all of our neighborhood recognizes the charming and friendly Xi Shi. But she has learned about the peculiarities of my family. Every time we show up, she'd produce something we love.

We always thought that the lady with such good looks and a bit of baby fat must be only in her early 20s. During a chat, she shocked us again by talking about her son. We soon got over the surprise, as many rural women wed early.

But it turned out that her son is already a teenager! My wife and I both gasped and stepped back.

"How old are you?" we asked.

"Nearly 40," she replied.

Back home, my fair lady gulped down the pork braised in brown sauce in silent determination, as if the dish contained the secrets to everlasting beauty.

HU XUDONG
(May 9, 2007)

71. The impossible dream of Beijing's new red chambers

A famous scene from *Dream of the Red Chamber* perfectly described China's rich-poor divide.

Peasant Granny Liu is flabbergasted at the extravagance of her rich relatives' 80-crab lunch. "I could feed my family for a year with this one lunch," she exclaimed.

Dream is one of China's four classic novels with insightful social commentary on the haves and have-nots — those who could afford to feast on crab banquets and those who could not.

China has been in the grip of crab season, and the little nippers are as expensive as ever.

My friend Zhu Li went online to buy a special variety and was quoted 160 yuan (about $21) for two, plus a delivery fee. It was out of her reach.

The magazine editorial assistant earns 2,800 yuan a month. After paying 1,200 yuan rent for her small room in a tiny Beijing apartment and forking out for other living expenses, she is left with 300 yuan a week. Her crab meal would have blown half her weekly budget.

Last weekend, I met her at one of the capital's leafy parks, which was kind of like the peaceful gardens in *Dream*. She was with her boyfriend, who is nicknamed ET, because of his big head, according to Zhu's colleague Liu, who joined us. Sam,

25, an enthusiastic karaoke singer and wannabe pop star, also tagged along.

Like the characters in *Dream*, we spent the afternoon enjoying one another's company and the glorious autumn sunshine. We took photos of the yellow leaves against the deep blue sky, and when Sam posed for photos, he strutted a cover model pose. He took it very seriously, and we all laughed at him.

We later drove dodgem cars and laughed more.

We walked along a lake and hard sunlight cast a mirror of sparkling color across the water. A dozen shades of light green danced on the ripples to the sound of flutes played by a musical group who had gathered under trees. Old men wrote calligraphy with water brushes. Crowds gathered to watch them.

I looked up and noticed a red-colored block of luxury apartments looming over the park, and I queried the price. About 2 million yuan, was the consensus. "I reckon they're eating crabs tonight," we said.

Afterward, we visited Zhu's shoebox of an apartment and crowded into her bedroom, which became a mini-dining room. She cooked a marvelous meal of pork and potato, green vegetables, bread and a tasty soup. ET brought some special sauce from his home province of Shandong.

We bought the food from the markets, and our little banquet for five cost about 20 yuan. Two crabs each would have cost 800 yuan.

On the way, we stopped by a real estate agent front window and I noticed a picture of the apartment building overlooking the park. I remembered its distinctive red color. "More than 3 million yuan," the agent said.

I watched Zhu, ET, Liu and Sam stare at the picture of a luxury apartment that these young 20-something Beijingers would probably never own.

As I watched my friends hold the 20-yuan bags of groceries and gaze into that real estate window, I could tell what was in their minds. They were dreaming of a red chamber.

PATRICK WHITELEY
(Nov 8, 2007)

72. Hearts warm the winter chill

It is said, "the road to hell is paved with good intentions".

Sometimes, this seems to be all too true. While teaching English in Zhuhai, Guangdong province, for several years, I noticed an old couple whose workplace was my gate.

They worked so hard, all days and all hours. They collected rubbish and brought it to the spot near my entrance where they sorted, stacked and bundled their finds. Every time I passed by, they would flash big toothless grins as we exchanged greetings.

What really caught my eye was that during the blistering summer days, the old fellow would be crouched in the shade of the gate, reading. Reading is my own passion, so I felt even more kinship.

After a year or so, a younger, and equally hardworking couple joined them and, to my delight, they brought along their little toddler boy. I'd say "baby" and he'd laugh and say "*nai nai*" (granny), then jump in my arms. As I dearly missed my own grandsons, he filled a spot in my heart.

When winter came, I loved finding some warm clothes for the little family. The young couple seemed adequately nourished and the boy was robust. But the old couple were thin as twigs, and I worried about them staying well. They were working people, not beggars, so I didn't give them money, only books and clothes as I would my own family.

Once when they went back to their hometown, they brought me back some of the best corned beef I've ever enjoyed.

Finally, I hit upon the idea of giving the "baby", who was now a happy boy, a red envelope for the New Year. When I left Zhuhai to live in Hangzhou, Zhejiang province, I made sure the amount would be enough to cushion them in the year ahead should the old couple get ill or they need something for the boy's first year of school.

Returning to Zhuhai to celebrate the Year of the Ox, I was thrilled to see the young couple still at their spot. We hugged and, without speaking each other's language, displayed our joy in seeing one another again. Through body language I learned that the elders were in the hometown with the boy.

On my last day there, I had a red envelope tucked in my pocket for the boy. The wife gestured that I should wait a minute. She rushed off and returned, to my horror, with a gigantic basket filled with brandy and wine and expensive cookies. I jumped back as if bitten, crying: "No, no!"

I had hoped to privately hand the envelope to her, but nothing stays private in China for long. Within minutes we had drawn a circle of interested and vocal bystanders.

I tried, to no avail, to explain that I couldn't take such things with me. A woman in the crowd who followed my body language, told my friend, in Cantonese, about the plane and my limitations. Of course, I was stricken that she had spent so much hard-earned money on the gift.

I was able to tuck the envelope in a pocket as I walked away. We both had tears in our eyes. My one and only consolation is that I put enough in the envelope to pay for the outrageously expensive gift and, since she probably can't return it, they can warm themselves through the rest of the winter with tots of good brandy they otherwise would have never tasted. I hope some of it finds its way to the old couple in their hometown.

SANDRA LEE
(Feb 24, 2009)

73. Mr Makeover colors our lives

On a freezing dark night, we arrived at the foot of our new apartment building.

It didn't take us long to realize that the security guard and a few passers-by were gazing up at our window. Xiao Shu, our decoration director, was leaning by the window and counting cash.

"Xiao Shu, everyone knows what you are doing," we joked. In the old days, showing off money was seen as rustic and asking for trouble.

Xiao Shu replied with his signature grin, his face shone red against the brightly lit green walls. Obviously, he had taken another "small sip" to celebrate the conclusion of his work in our decoration project.

Our painter Lao Wang and carpenter Xiao Guizi (or Small Cupboard) happily accepted their share of the bulk of cash from Xiao Shu, picked up their tight bundles of quilts and equipment, bade us adieu and headed home to rural Anhui province for the Spring Festival.

Getting train tickets has been impossible. They will endure days and nights of crowded bus rides for family reunions, where they'll be seen as the capable and rich, instead of powerless outsiders in the strange big city.

Over the years, we have become good friends with Xiao Shu, a bond that I believe is rare and surprisingly strong in this increasingly commercialized society.

We got to know him when a friend decorated her home. Xiao Shu quarreled with her almost daily. My friend is a perfectionist and habitually asked him to revise finished work. But he believed in simpler methods and less expensive materials.

Believing him to be a straightforward person like us, we asked him to paint our basement. He led us to an obscure decoration market and bargained for paint and tiles of good quality. But he refused to accept our payment.

Xiao Shu once ran his own decoration company but gave up when he lost 20,000 yuan ($2,750) to poor management. He'd rather personally handle all the work if the task is small. For big apartments, he rallies a team comprising carpenter, painter, electrician and others, all of whom come from the same village and dwell in rented shacks in Beijing's suburbs.

At the height of our decoration, half a dozen workers slept and cooked at the site. Their rapidfire dialect sounded like quarreling even though they were just discussing the shade of a green paint or the straightness of a line.

It seems eating is the paramount entertainment for them. Twice a week, they went shopping at a nearby rural market and came back with vegetables. They'd carefully smear salt on the ducks and dry them on the balcony. Eating duck could help clear away the dust they inhaled, says our painter, who has to polish the wall many times before applying paint.

Not everyone follows Xiao Shu's orders. One of our veteran carpenters, who cooked mouthwatering fish, always replied "impossible" to our requests. Once he refused to modify the ceiling, as curved lines took much more time to realize than straight ones.

Seeing that he couldn't persuade the carpenter, Xiao Shu grabbed a handsaw, climbed onto the ladder and started sawing the wooden structure. Suddenly, the saw broke in two. Everyone laughed heartily, including Xiao Shu, who used to be a handsome carpenter but has gained much weight over the past decade.

Coming from a family with scholars and officials in history, Xiao Shu dropped out of school during the "cultural revolution" (1966-76). Like many migrant workers in the country's metropolises, he works hard to support his two sons through university.

He has already made enough money to build a two-story house in his hometown. But his wife would rather cook for him in their rented flat in Beijing.

"I don't have much to worry about," he concluded, admiring our new ceiling before heading home.

LIU JUN
(Jan 16, 2008)

74. A finely wrought story

I was looking for wrought iron art when I bumped into a store in one of Beijing's immense home decoration centers that sells everything from Western-styled sofas to bright red lanterns adorned with ancient Chinese paintings.

"You'd better choose from our works on display, so the costs are lower," advised the young salesman in his early 20s. Unlike most other salespeople I've met, he spoke standard *putonghua*.

In just one minute, he sketched several patterns that we wanted in a notebook. Evidently, he has received at least basic training in the arts. But I couldn't help gazing at the single, nail-shaped earring shining in his left ear.

"For a pair of these, 50 yuan ($6.80)," he said, after we agreed on a leaf pattern in Arabic style, using a thick copper wire.

"Shouldn't we call the boss to make sure?" the young girl, who had been silent all this time, timidly asked the young man.

"There's no need," he said, waving his hand.

As we discussed how to fashion another pair of bronze ornaments, the young man looked up and uttered: "Here comes my boss. You'd better talk with the real expert."

A balding man in his 50s barged in. To my surprise and amusement, the young man greeted him as "Dad".

The Dad-boss sat down with much gravity, and we heard that the leaf pattern would cost 100 yuan per pair.

"But your son just offered half that price," I protested. "We should've settled the deal before you came back."

"He doesn't know the business well," the older man said in a thick Beijing accent. "But if you had inked the contract and he had only charged you 1 yuan, I would have honored the deal."

Embarrassed, the young man pretended to fix a dangling ornament on the door. The old man seemed to sense his son's silence and pointed at a set of refined clothes hangers. "My son created the whole set. It'd look great on the wall," he said.

But was it really worth adding all these metal elements to my already crowded home?

Seeing my hesitation, the old man remarked: "You will forget about the price soon. After all, you could spend the same sum on a single meal with your friends."

I accepted this. But when I tried to cut down the costs by opting for a thinner material, the old man was indignant.

"They are different materials. If I agree to do the work for you, I must ensure it is the best."

After living in the nation's capital for more than 10 years, I've noticed that local residents — people who are at least second-generation — are proud, whether they are taxi drivers or acoustic system dealers.

Many literary works have discussed this phenomenon, and some social critics attribute this pride to Beijing's long history as the nation's political and cultural center.

Sometimes this can be annoying to newcomers, especially those from smaller cities or the countryside. But more often than not, I find local people very honest and lovable.

"Well, I'll trust you to complete the contract. I must hurry to the hospital," the old man told his son. Then, he turned to me and said: "What a life! Both of my parents are in their 80s. The old man is paralyzed, and my mother fell ill last night."

The family has been in the wrought iron trade for decades. The old man has led his team of a dozen workers to Shanghai and even to Africa to decorate gates and windows, and make tables with marble surfaces.

Following the market rule, I paid 100 yuan and signed a contract. Then, I left, departing with a deeper understanding of the immense city I now call home.

LIU JUN
(Dec 20, 2007)

75. Digging in on Labor Day

"Do you want to be a farmer for two days?" a friend asked me just before the May Day holiday. "Why not?" I thought. It must be a lot of fun. I happily accepted, hoping to have a real Labor Day.

The farmland she mentioned is actually the empty garden of her villa in Yanqing, a mountainous district some 80 km northwest of Beijing, close to the Badaling Great Wall.

It's a 666-square-meter courtyard. The garden surrounding the two-story house is unkempt and wild. We planned to plant two peach, two apricot and two apple trees. Unfortunately, we were told we were two weeks late for tree planting. We have to wait until next April.

Quite disappointed, we stood in the courtyard, watching the couple next door plowing their lands, some of which already showed signs of green.

"You can grow corn," said the woman next door. "I have the seeds." She came back with a bowl of pink kernels.

Finally, we had something to do. I volunteered to dig the holes, thinking it would be quite easy to use the spade. The first hole was perfect and the second okay, but I almost broke the spade with the third one, as it hit a rock.

I felt beads of perspiration on my brow. The digging that followed was a mix of the difficult and the easy. I managed to dig 40 holes, each big enough for two seeds.

Since we had nothing more to do, we decided to take a stroll. It is interesting to see people busily digging everywhere — either inside the courtyard or in the open areas.

The site of the villas used to be a small village at the foot of Mount Senmao with limited arable land. Several years ago, the village head decided to develop the land as real estate to bring the villagers out of poverty. He built 500 villas and several apartment buildings.

The villagers moved into a four-story apartment building and enjoy free housing in addition to receiving some money. They no longer work in the fields. Instead, the men are busy with the villas' interior decoration. The women and elderly people enjoy sitting and chatting in front of their building.

"I find it most interesting to watch those city people doing farm work," said an old man in his 70s, surnamed Zhao. "Look at that courtyard," he said, pointing to a villa in the corner. "He has too many things in his field."

We realized that we knew the owner, an IT manager.

"I don't care about the results," the owner, Huang Sheng, said. "I enjoy the sweating, and the aches and pains." He held a spade and wiped his brow with his dusty T-shirt.

In his 333-sq-m courtyard, he has planted 16 trees, including apple, peach, pear and persimmon saplings.

I stood on a piece of brick and didn't know where to move my feet. It seems something is growing on every available patch of land.

Huang proudly pointed to the corner by the iron fence and said he is growing sweet melons and beans. He said the place where I was standing was for peanuts, although all I could see in the yard was one patch of green onions.

Although he still has his city belly, his face has taken on a healthy tan. "Come autumn, you may get something," Huang said. I am sure it will be one busy garden.

LIN JINGHUA
(May 8, 2008)

76. Same old village, brand new livelihoods

A solitary farmer makes his way up the track with some kind of crude tree-pruning implement resting on his shoulder. Another chops wood outside his home with an axe that looks like it came out of the Stone Age.

Hens cluck around his feet, and their pecking and the splintering of wood are the only sounds in a rural scene that has probably not changed much for hundreds of years.

But despite the appearance of a yesteryear world out here in Beijing's northern outskirts, I've noticed a remarkable transformation since I rented a courtyard here.

Policy changes and the easing of restrictions have meant a change in lifestyles that none of them could have imagined 30 years ago.

Wang Shuhua is one of hundreds of fruit farmers who have opened *nongjiayuan* (family countryside guesthouses) where city dwellers stay at weekends when they go to climb hills and gawp at skies that really are blue and really do have fluffy, white clouds.

Years ago, opening one's home to outsiders was strictly forbidden, but now, many households are enjoying a dual means of income.

Wang tells me his son, Wang Haidong, started the guesthouse. "People come from Beijing to stay. They love the fresh air." As the family also grows fruit, Wang says life is "much easier than it was years ago".

Down the hill, a red sign directs weekenders to Wang Chunlian's guesthouse, where flowers blossomed in the yard as early as the end of winter.

Wang opened her guesthouse 10 years ago, and, since then, dozens of others have sprung up. "Competition is stiff now. Lots of farmers do it because it's nicer work and pays better. But I have regulars who only come to my house. We don't just depend on guests. We still have our land. We all grow fruit and corn, and other vegetables."

Chatting to some farmers near some rocks, I learn more. What looks like a hillside scattered with various trees is actually a hillside divided into lots that are worked by individual families. The boundaries aren't physically there, but each farmer knows exactly which bit is his as if a grid of white lines is painted over the hillside.

"See that tree over there with the crooked branch?" one burnt-faced farmer, taking a break atop a pile of boulders, points out.

"I can expect to get 100 *jin* (50 kg) off that tree come autumn. See the bent one next to it? That marks the boundary between my land and Lao Wang's. His bit stretches over there just to the brow of the hill, and then it's Old Wife Xiu's. She mainly grows lychees."

His friend explains: "Our land hasn't changed, but what we can do with it has. We used to be told exactly what to grow and where we could sell it. We had to give some of it to the government before we could sell the rest. And we had to take it to the market. We couldn't sell it in our own village. Now, we grow what we want and sell it wherever we like."

Farmers can also sublet and transfer the use of their land to others. Those who sublet can join others to form larger companies, increasing farming efficiency.

Most of those in my village farm their own plots but with less of a tax burden. "We had to pay 50 yuan a year in taxes, but that's gone now."

As my son and I stroll up the tiny village's "main street", we stop in a small restaurant. The looks from diners and the owners are those of recognition.

"We know you. You're that foreigner, the one who's just rented old Hu's house up on the hill."

"Just here for one night again? Rented a car to get here again? And this must be your son. Four years old, isn't he? Did Lao Feng sort out those beds for you?"

I guess there are some things about village life that never change.

DEBBIE MASON
(June 10, 2009)

77. Saying goodbye at a traditional funeral

We run a guesthouse in a small village near Guilin, Guangxi Zhuang autonomous region, and integrating into rural life has been one of our main interests.

Recently, the father of our night guard passed away. The bangs of fireworks heralded the start of the funeral, on a day that rained continuously, causing floods — unusual in the dry season.

The immediate family stayed with the body for nearly two days, and various rituals were carried out. They were signs of respect and a way of saying farewell. Possibly a vital chance for the Chinese involved to hold on to some of their rich cultural heritage.

Bowls of rice and steamed pigs' legs were put in front of the heavy, wooden coffin, as well as a live chicken with its feet tied. Close family members wore off-white linen coats, hurriedly made for the occasion.

The firecrackers exploded all day and night, scaring away the bad spirits. The musicians played their tin flutes and drums. Dragon dancers followed a rhythm so as to protect the dead man on his path to the afterlife.

When it was our turn to offer sympathies to the family, we stopped at the local corner shop to buy a red envelope (*hongbao*) and put some notes in to contribute to the funeral costs, as well as buying incense sticks and paper money. Then, we stepped into the makeshift tent.

Michael, my husband, stood in front of the coffin and lit a candle, which he placed on an upside-down rice bowl. He repeated the procedure with a bunch of incense sticks and let our two boys copy him. I went last.

We folded some paper money, set fire to it and placed it facing the altar on the sandy floor, where it quickly turned to ashes. The smoke from the burned donations was carried away by the wind.

Lastly, we bowed a few times out of respect to the deceased and shook hands with his family members. A strong bond connected us with these people.

Luo Jie

We were also invited to the funeral's evening meal and felt honored. Mourning, for us, is a private affair, but this invitation seemed like a sign of acceptance and trust.

The funeral party never left the body of the dead man. There was plenty of time for tears. In the morning, the coffin was closed and tied up with the off-white cloth ribbons previously worn by the family. The rain stopped. Half a dozen strong men lifted up the box and carried it slowly down the street toward the mountain.

Two youngsters walked in front of the procession. They held fireworks and let them off every few meters, leaving a trail of red paper along the way. The musicians marched at the back. The lion dancers gave a final performance.

The many hours without sleep, the weeping, the noise, smoke and alcohol drunk at the funeral had exhausted the dead man's family. They were at the end of their strength. They bowed in front of their beloved deceased for the last time and broke down.

A small girl, carried on the back of her mother, waved to us. A wire construction was put on the coffin, crowned by a colorful paper bird that would fly away with the spirit of the dead and become part of the circle of life.

NADINE HUDSON
(July 29, 2009)

6. SURPRISE, SURPRISE

78. Tipping me over the edge

Tip or don't tip? Whichever I choose, it's wrong.

When I lived in the United States, the size of the tip you were expected to leave was virtually the first thing they would tell you when you walked through the door.

"Hello, sir. Gratuity here is 12 percent. Can I take your coat?" some smarmy waiter would say.

"Take my coat? For 12 percent, you can do my taxes!" I'd reply. I'd laugh, but my little joke was usually met with only confusion. There's no messing with tips in the US. It's strict.

In China, it's different. If I even mention the word "tip" here the server gives me a steely look that says: "Just try it, Mister!"

My first bizarre tipping experience came when I was traveling in South China, long before I moved to Beijing. At the time, I would stop off in random places to "get off the beaten track" and test my Chinese-language skills.

One such place was Chaozhou, a relatively small city in southern Guangdong province. I'd only stayed one day, and, before I boarded the afternoon bus to my next destination, I settled down for lunch in a Japanese restaurant.

The food was good and the waitresses had been kind in putting up with my poor Chinese for an hour or so, so I left 20 yuan as thanks.

One minute later, now outside and walking away from the restaurant, I heard an almighty commotion behind me. I thought maybe someone had robbed a bank and was being pursued by the police. Perhaps a thief had snatched an old lady's purse and was being hounded by a have-a-go hero.

No. I was the prey in this desperate pursuit. When the waitress caught up with me, she shoved the 20-yuan note into my hand and simply said sorry.

"*Wo gei nimen* (I left it for the staff)," I argued, but to no avail. She simply repeated her apology and disappeared down the street.

Some would have taken this as a lesson that "to tip is to err". I saw it as a challenge.

I simply employed more stealth in my approach — hiding the cash under plates and bowls, and running for the first 500 meters once outside to put a good distance between the staff and me.

It made me feel warm inside knowing I was beating the system. But the rush faded after a while, and it just wasn't enough. I needed confrontation. So, during a recent trip to Qingdao, I brazenly left 20 yuan for all to see on the table of a pizzeria and walked out like nothing had happened. Cue the frantic waitress.

I refused to acknowledge she was chasing me until she was right behind me. "You left this," she said. "Sorry, but we can't accept it."

"But it's not mine," I said, with the most innocent look I could muster.

"Errrr, but you were sitting at that table, and it was there when you left. It must be yours. We can't take it."

"Nope, not mine. I've already got a 20-yuan note," I pulled one out of my pocket to show her. I turned to walk away, allowing myself to bask in the glow of my first real victory.

But I had counted my chickens too early. With the speed of a bullet, she slipped the note into the back pocket of my jeans and made off at a terrific pace. I could only applaud my wily opponent. "You've won this round, my girl, but I'll be back!" I yelled.

The following week I was back in Beijing. Not quite ready for round two, I had ordered a pizza delivery to my home and was anxiously waiting when there was a knock at my door. The young motorbike rider handed me my pizza, I handed him the cash and we went our separate ways.

"Did you tip him?" asked my girlfriend as the first slice approached my lips.

"No," I said. "I had the exact change."

"You big meany," she blasted. "Always tip a delivery boy!"

CRAIG MCINTOSH

(Aug 19, 2009)

79. Honestly, try fibbing some time

Who coined the phrase "Honesty is always the best policy"?

Maybe it was Confucius. It wouldn't surprise me, as every Chinese person seems to strictly adhere to the principle.

Honesty is not always the best policy. In some situations, in fact, it is the worst policy — or at least a distant second to the policy of "keeping your big mouth shut".

After my mother stepped off the plane in Beijing and we were on our way home in the taxi, I took the opportunity to give her the briefing all expats no doubt give their loved ones in this situation.

"First, Mother, don't look at how the taxi driver is driving. Look out the window and admire the buildings and bridges (as much as you can on the Jichang airport expressway), but just don't look at the traffic," I told her. She immediately looked at the traffic.

"Second, don't worry about the spitting. They are spitting with you, not at you, OK? And third, they don't mean to offend you; they are just being honest."

She chuckled at this last one but soon stopped when she saw the deathly serious glint in my eye.

Mum understood me perfectly just a few days later. She and my girlfriend had somehow missed the exit to the Summer Palace and were wandering for some time before an old Chinese gentleman came up and asked if they happened to be lost.

"How did you notice us?" asked my Chinese girlfriend. "It was impossible to miss you," he said, pointing at my mother, adding: "She's so big and fat, like a giant!"

My mother is a full-bodied woman, one might say, and unashamedly so. She also, thankfully, has a good sense of humor. As she speaks not a word of Chinese, she would have been none-the-wiser had the old man not used such extravagant hand gestures to make his point.

Days later, the three of us headed to Qingdao for a relaxing weekend on the beach. My girlfriend had booked us a unique accommodation, which was a couple's home, the spare rooms of which they let out to travelers at a very reasonable rate.

It was fantastic, a wonderful change to staying in a cold, unfriendly hotel. The couple, a South Korean man and his Chinese wife, brewed some of the best tea we'd ever tasted. And, although their level of English was limited, they made my mother feel at home.

Late on the first night, once my mother had gone to bed and we four stayed up drinking beer, our hostess leaned across to me and said: "*Ni mama hen ke ai*!" (Your mother is so cute!)

"Thank you," I said, almost knowing a heavy dose of honesty was on the horizon.

"Yeah," she continued. "She's so big and fat, great to cuddle. And we love her smile, with her big rabbit teeth. My husband says she reminds him of his own mother. That's why we keep buying her cakes; she must get hungry a lot."

My other half was more than happy to pass on this information to my mother the next morning. It didn't stop her from eating the cakes, however.

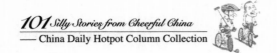

Back in Beijing, my mother settled down for a coffee with my girlfriend to ask her intentions. She extolled the virtues of being a good wife but explained it can also be hard, especially in the old days when women did all the washing up and cleaning around the house.

"That doesn't bother me," my beloved said. "I'm young and able. I can handle all that."

"So is that to say I'm old and unable?" my mother retorted jokingly, not expecting a response.

"Yes," came the all-too-honest reply. "You're far too old."

It had occurred to me that honesty is maybe not just the best policy but the ONLY policy for Chinese. Then I remembered the Silk Market.

"It's all 100-percent silk, handsome man, really!" Yeah, right.

CRAIG MCINTOSH

(July 28, 2009)

80. Swimming with the Beijing icebergs

The Chinese can sometimes be a weird bunch.

In summer, the men love pulling their T-shirts up to expose their mighty bellies and in winter, they enjoy stripping down to their swim trunks and jumping into frozen lakes. Women take the icy plunge, too.

Water temps drop to about 3C. Considering the body's normal temperature is about 37C, this icy plunge is one almighty shock to the system. If you stayed in for 20 minutes you'd probably die, but a 3-minute experience is supposed to be euphoric. That's why these swimmers do it.

After a moment of major discomfort, they feel very invigorated. The icy water contracts the skin, and like a sponge, squeezes out all the toxins. Blood rushes to the heart and is drained from all the limbs. The heart pumps like a racing car engine. The swimmer climbs out of the water and towels off but doesn't feel cold.

They don't feel anything — their feet or the cold air on their skin — because the nerve endings are numb. Then the magic happens. Blood starts circulating around the body and the central nervous system shouts: Hallelujah! These winter swimmers attain a natural high.

There's a joke that fits this scenario like a woolen glove. Why does a fool hit his hand with a hammer? Because it feels so good when he stops.

We don't need to jump into an icy lake to appreciate how cold it gets in China. The Chinese winter wind can certainly pound a fair-weathered foreigner like a sledgehammer.

The good news is the pains of winter are nearly over. The Spring Festival is here and is not only adding warmth to the hearts of a family-focused nation but also signaling the beginning of warmer weather. Hello sunshine!

However, for some strange reason, I'm going to miss winter. I took to it like a Peking duck to water. I enjoyed it like those Beijing polar bears who enjoyed jumping into frozen lakes because the best thing about freezing is the joy of thawing out.

A typical winter night for me went like this: I scurry from the warm cab and get savagely attacked by the night wind. Banging my feet on the ground, I dash to my apartment. My ears are numb and haven't stung so much since I heard my first Peking Opera.

The walk home turns to a trot and soon I'm leaping in giant strides to give Liu Xiang a run for his yuan.

My freezing hands fumble for the keys and soon I'd be inside my centrally heated apartment thawing-out. My bliss begins. I can feel my body temperature rising and enjoy blood flowing back to my hands, my legs and, best of all, my ears. Ear we go, ear we go, ear we go.

I've been exposed to a few -5C nights and never imagined adapting to it. But handled it, I have.

They say fools rush in where angels fear to tread, and my mother in Sydney thought I was a crazy fool to live in China during winter. Mum is basking in 32C heat and recently asked me: "Why in the heck do you enjoy freezin' your noggin off?"

Because, Mom, it feels so good when it stops.

PATRICK WHITELEY
(Feb 13, 2007)

81. **Blessing of the *Golden Flower***

The *Seinfeld* TV series was a huge hit in the 1990s thanks to its cast of self-centered New Yorkers and their funny observations about life.

One episode starts with Jerry and George sitting in their favorite diner. George is flicking through the New York Times and spots an article about China.

"Ah Jerry, don't they know that anything about China is a page turner?" He quickly flicks the page and the pre-recorded TV audience laugh fires up. He's saying: OK. It's the world's biggest country — but who cares? What the hell has it got to do with me?

That episode was made about 10 years ago, and, as we all know, the New York Times, and the rest of the world's media, has ignored George's editorial advice. Editors in the West know what their customers want, and all eyes and ears are on China. They're even on its historical epic movies, which are the butt of many Chinese jokes.

My Aunty Delie from Indianapolis in the US shocked me recently when she revealed her favorite movie of 2006 was *Curse of the Golden Flower*.

Delie lives smack-dab in Middle America and watched Zhang Yimou's Tang Dynasty (AD 618-907) epic sipping a Diet Coke and munching on popcorn in a mid-western mall. This was not a San Francisco foreign film festival or New York's Greenwich Village. This was the US heartland and as mainstream as it gets. What's she doing watching a foreign-language film? Doesn't she know that China is a page-turner?

"It was subtitled, but I didn't care. I absolutely loved it!" my aunty exclaimed. "The costumes were amazing, the colors were powerful, the acting was marvelous, the emperor (Chow Yun-fat) was brilliant, and the story was so true."

The story? I told her the narratives of China's big blockbusters, such as *The Curse*, *The Banquet* and *The Promise*, are regarded by many Chinese as their major weakness. Locals feel their big-name directors have lost touch with the mainstream, and focus too much on style and not enough on substance.

But my 55-year-old Australian/American aunty was riveted by the story and the unique way in which it was told.

"The emperor's power and greed took away everything he really loved — that's so true," she said.

My aunt is going through a nasty court case, involving a former business partner, and Zhang's costume epic weaved its way into her heart. I told her locals didn't think the story was relevant. "But it was relevant to me," Delie said. "Greed will ruin a man. Don't I know it."

I was quick to jump on the I-hate-big-Chinese-epic-movies bandwagon and watched *The Curse* again with new eyes. Aunty Delie was right.

Under the overwhelming colors, sword fights and dazzling costumes was a story of substance. *The Curse* wasn't as cursed as I'd first thought. Next year, Zhang Yimou will help stage the opening ceremony of the Olympic Games and if you want a sneak peak of what it may look like, check out *The Curse*. It is available on DVD.

Even if you think it is cursed, there's a good chance your overseas aunty will like it and might find it to be a more interesting gift then a pair of chopsticks.

PATRICK WHITELEY
(Feb 28, 2007)

82. What the *fengshui* master revealed

The bald-headed *fengshui* master examined my palms, studied my face, noted my time of birth, stared into my eyes and then slowly shuffled back behind his table in the quiet little Lijiang restaurant. He sipped his tea, leaned across the table and asked: "Do you trust me?"

The master had returned from an important project in Shangri-la. The world-famous city's world-famous giant statue of Buddha had not received a *fengshui* checkup in 200 years, and the local government had hired the master to look at the spatial arrangement around the statue. After two centuries, the flow of energy (*qi*) around Buddha needed a little unclogging. After fixing Buddha, the master now had his sights set on me.

I was living in very interesting times, indeed.

I met my *fengshui* master in Lijiang, an enchanting, 700-year-old city with streets paved in cobblestone and snow-capped mountains looming over traditional tiled rooftops. Many argued it was Shangri-La, the place mentioned in James Hamilton's 1933 novel, *The Lost Horizons*. Hamilton described a mountaintop paradise where people lived in harmony, reveling in learning and profound inner peace. In 2002, Zhongdian, in northwestern Yunnan province and three hours' drive from Lijiang, was officially declared to be Shangri-La.

The *fengshui* master had been telling me about his craft, and I asked him if he could do to me what he did to the Buddha in Shangri-la. I couldn't resist.

"Do you trust me?" he asked again with a very serene smile. "It won't work if you don't trust me."

I felt like he was using a sales line, and I was a bit reluctant to say I trusted someone I had only known for about 15 minutes.

But this gentle soul was not asking for money. He was just being friendly and sharing his knowledge.

It's the sort of thing that happens to foreigners all across China every day. For me it was interesting China experience No 769. These moments are the reason I came.

So I said the magic words: "I trust you."

He laughed, pushed away his tea and ordered a beer. I later discovered he loved a quiet beer ... or eight.

The 50-something master said I looked stressed and should learn to love myself more. He said my face was balanced, and there was no need to be so ambitious.

Good things would come my way when I was ready for them.

To be ready for them, I needed to live more in the moment. He said life was about balance. When good things come, enjoy them, embrace them and get excited for one minute, no more. Then go back to a peaceful, neutral zone. When bad stuff happens, feel it, wail, but only for one minute, no more.

Then return to the balanced core. Return to the moment.

It was all good, and soon I said goodbye. I wanted to give the *fengshui* master something in return but what do you give someone who wants nothing, and knows the meaning of everything?

What do you give a man who just fixed the Buddha of Shangri-la's *qi*?

I bought him another beer.

PATRICK WHITELEY
(Aug 29, 2007)

83. Losing a perfect job opportunity

My friend Xiao Wang should have scored a 40,000-yuan ($5,256) a month job as a sales director at a top US company. Instead he became yet another victim of the East-meets-West culture clash.

The American company was a major international player and was hunting for a top sales manager who could fire up its new Chinese operations. China-born, US-educated Xiao Wang was more than qualified, having worked in the US in the same industry but living most of his life in China. He knew the local market well.

The mid-30s Beijinger is a naturally charming fellow, and after dining with him a few times I could understand why he had carved out a successful sales career. He is a great listener, and always gives his undivided attention to whoever is speaking. He has the knack of making you feel special and rarely speaks about himself. He also has an X factor, which is only discovered in a face-to-face meeting.

The US firm flew Xiao Wang to Shanghai for the main interview and the feedback was positive. Xiao Wang had one more hurdle, a final telephone meeting with the Asia Pacific sales director, who was based in the US.

After the hookup, Xiao Wang felt confident. Interestingly, the interviewer did not ask many questions, however, Xiao Wang believed it was simply a confirmation call.

His interpretation was way off the mark. The American boss later said that Xiao Wang did not have the drive and passion to lead a new business.

This was the classic West-meets-East cultural dilemma in which the aggressive meets the passive.

I have found that many Chinese are not direct. My Chinese friends tell me that speaking your mind in front of others may cause disharmony to the group. Although there are exceptions to this rule, and the younger generation is becoming more forthright, many Chinese still believe that it is better to agree face-to-face and negotiate afterwards than to blatantly disagree at a meeting.

Westerners may consider this indirectness deceptive.

The US sales director may have been expecting a typical "go-getter" sales guy like himself. He may have been expecting the candidate to behave like he once had in previous job interviews.

He wanted a sales manager who oozed confidence and was powered by aggression. He wanted someone who was willing to knock down doors and explain why he was the right man for the job. Xiao Wang was not on the same page. He was waiting for questions and expected the mood and pace of the conversation to be dictated by the interviewer.

Body language expert Albert Mehrabian found that only 7 percent of communication was verbal (words only) and 38 percent vocal (tone of voice, inflection and other sounds). More than half of the communication process — 55 percent — was non-verbal, including body language, facial expressions and gestures.

If only the American big shot had enjoyed a hotpot with Xiao Wang, he would have met the real man and would have probably hired him and guaranteed his China operations' success.

PATRICK WHITELEY
(Dec 5, 2007)

84. *"Chi fan le ma"* — always a safe question

Chi fan le ma (have you eaten?) is what many Chinese ask after saying *ni hao* and is one of the most civilized and meaningful small-talk topics ever developed. Opinions about food, no matter who you are, are always interesting and never start fights.

Money, religion and politics have long been taboo topics of conversation in many circles of society because they are considered too personal and often cause division.

Boasting about your appreciating property value is not appreciated by renters and pontificating about a particular political viewpoint can polarize a party.

In 2007, money, religion and politics are probably the most talked about subjects on the World Wide Web and are not ignored in China by a long shot.

I'm often asked: "How much do you make?" It halts me in my tracks. I don't feel comfortable about sharing my gross monthly worth so I used to make up a figure, which was high enough to be realistic for a foreigner. My lie never worked.

My alleged salary was always dismissed with a *"Bu shi* (no way). You get more than that!" I now shrug my shoulders and jokingly answer: "Never enough."

This quip seems to be the universally accepted answer for all workers, even the super rich like me, ha.

US billionaire JD Rockefeller was once asked how much was enough. His response: "A little bit more."

Chinese often ask about my religion. My friend Qing Ma says all foreigners are Christians, aren't they? In the West, when someone probes about religion, it's often the lead-up to an ear bashing. The inquisitor only wants to know my viewpoint on God, the universe and everything, so they can tell me how I've got it wrong. What they don't understand is their opinion about me is none of my business.

My Chinese friends who ask about spirituality really don't care what I believe. They are just curious. According to them, everything is everybody's business.

I tell them my philosophy. Love many, trust few and paddle your own canoe.

"But what's a canoe?" they ask.

Politics? Some people are Left wing and others are Right wing. I am more of a chili chicken wing guy myself, which leads me to my favorite talking point. Have you eaten yet?

Food, glorious food. I love chewing the fat on this tasty topic.

When I first started working in a Chinese office, I really wanted to know what everybody was talking about besides work. Last night's TV show? Juicy gossip about Gong Li? Maybe Yao Ming's last NBL game?

I later discovered they were mostly talking about food. How long do you marinate an egg plant? The correct water measure for boiling rice? And have you eaten yet?

The expression *"Chi fan le ma?"* is very easy to remember, if you use my little trick. Remember that really catchy *Sesame Street* song *Manamana*?

The only words are ma na ma na — du du de du-du. Replace ma na ma na with *chi fan le ma*, and you'll always have something interesting to say in Chinese. "*Chi fan le ma* — du du de du-du."

I'm going to pitch my song to the Olympic Games organizers. What a great anthem for the opening ceremony, with Gong Li and Yao Ming leading the parade!

On that note, I've got to go. My chili chicken wings are getting cold.

PATRICK WHITELEY

(Jan 24, 2007)

85. Mechanics of the bare-belly radiator

One of the best ways to utterly dampen the cheerful mood of a friendly dinner party is to serve up the subject of global warming. What a party pooper!

"The end is nigh, the sky is falling, the temperatures are soaring, the oceans are rising, the floods will wash us all away and, excuse me ... could you pass the soy sauce?"

As summer starts to sizzle in the Middle Kingdom, the warmer weather, for some, prompts gloomy discussion of the world's pending doom.

For me, a Chinese summer is not a bummer. It is a season of intriguing and spectacular sights, the first of which are those absolutely fabulous bellies that parade the streets with pride.

The rising mercury forces T-shirts to rise, too, exposing some of the best bellies in the world as they bounce and jiggle. I especially like the big, fat Buddha-style bellies, blubbering around with purpose and poise.

The art of baring one's belly is not just an old man's game. It is practiced by men of all ages. I was gobsmacked to see a really hip 20-something guy bare his belly right in front of me.

He was wearing torn designer jeans, Elton John-style monster sunglasses, moccasins and a skin-tight bright orange singlet. As we were about to pass on the footpath, he rolled up his singlet and bingo!

From my experience, the barebelly cooling technique works best when walking. The whole process functions the same way a car's radiator chills out the engine.

The big bellies are the best. Girllike bellies, such as David Beckham's taut and trim tummy, are very hard to stomach. Some may say the Beckham belly is "ab fab", but I call it an absolute disgrace. Many football navel gazers support my view; they all say the soccer superstar lacks guts.

Another interesting summer outdoor practice, which I have rarely seen anywhere else, is the donning of pajamas in broad daylight. I saw an elderly couple strolling down the sidewalk in their flannels, and it was a real head-turner. I saw another, sitting cross-legged at the front of his hairdressing salon, wearing only his pajama bottoms at 4:30 pm.

In the West, if people wander the daytime streets in their PJs, many would call the police. Concerned citizens may think the curious wander had escaped from some mental hospital.

But I don't know why many of us Westerners think like that. Pajamas are one of the most comfortable kinds of clothing, and my recent observations have made me rethink my clothing code standards.

If I had my way, I'd wear pajamas all day and night. I can jump straight out of bed, walk out the door and go to work. If it gets a bit chilly, I'll put on a dressing gown and some slippers. But this is nothing new.

The ancient Chinese wore this outfit as their normal clobber, as did the Romans and the Greeks. And all these pajama-wearing guys knew how to throw excellent dinner parties.

I'm not a history expert, but I am sure of one thing. They didn't bore their dinner party guests senseless with talk of global warming.

PATRICK WHITELEY

(May 31, 2007)

86. The good news of rediscovering ritual

I think I am pretty adaptable.

I lived in Japan many years ago and felt that, when I moved to China to work as a teacher, I was prepared to find a vastly different world than the Hawaiian island home I'd left behind. But I seriously missed one ritual I had maintained all my life — reading the newspaper with my morning cup of coffee. Real coffee, not those horrible instant packets. A newspaper in English, not in Chinese. Neither was available, and I felt both losses keenly.

After a few years of having access to only an occasional paper from Hong Kong, the local China Post kiosk began to carry the China Daily. I immediately made an arrangement to have one saved for me every day. I now had a local source for real coffee and was delighted to reinstate my beloved morning cuppa and paper.

I began to clip items that would inform my students and began to be on the lookout for those that would instigate discussion. Most articles I clip are used for classroom reading. We cover new vocabulary and then discuss the topic.

Students in China, in general, do not like to have opposing opinions, so it often was slow going. But I've pressed on, because I believe that China needs people who can think "out of the box" and bring fresh ideas to the table.

I'm backed up by none other than President Hu Jintao. Several years ago, I began reading in the China Daily of his calls for China to become an "innovation nation". In a speech about rebuilding the Party, he said: "Emancipating the mind is a magic instrument." I couldn't agree more.

Dialogue and discourse, and the ability to see many sides of an issue, are crucial to arriving at good, and more creative, decisions. It also is a requisite if China is to stop copying and embark on more innovative projects and businesses.

On almost any topic covered in our textbooks, I have pertinent articles, and pictures and cartoons, with which I cover the board. Students learn that they don't have to labor over every word. They can get the gist and move on.

I encourage them to read a bit in each section. To be well informed is the best way to encourage conversation with English-speaking foreigners and leave a good impression of China's citizens. If they don't give a fig for sports and are not in business, knowing the current top stories will allow them to enter into conversations. And if they can't actually contribute much information, they can at least ask informed questions.

I try to instill a desire in my students to be well informed on current events and to love to read the newspaper. I am gradually accepting that most of them will not have the inky fingers of the true newspaper aficionados of my generation. They will more likely get online.

But it all leads to creating minds that are curious about the world we live in.

I have watched the China Daily make significant changes to create a newspaper that is well worth reading. I was thrilled on the day I saw a color photo on the cover!

I follow trends both here and abroad from my daily reading. I am interested in politics and have greatly appreciated the increasingly transparent reporting and the presentation of conflicting ideas. The coverage of the first space flight and the Sichuan earthquake was gripping as well as informative.

Have I converted anyone? Hard to say.

As a teacher we are only able to plant seeds. We don't often have the luxury of knowing how many blooms there are later, although some have been kind enough to tell me they now read the China Daily as a way to keep up their English and to be informed.

I hope it's true, because I'd like to spread the simple joy of reading the paper while sipping a cup of one's favorite brew. Nourishment for mind and body, all in one delightful daily ritual.

SANDRA LEE

(March 4, 2009)

87. How trinkets tell 10-second stories

Since my friends and family can't visit China themselves, I try to bring China to them — at least, all of the country I can cram into two suitcases.

The usual gifts — chopsticks, Great Wall T-shirts, calligraphy, scroll paintings, silk kites, tea sets — tend to reinforce their vision of a land where people eat food with sticks and build magnificent walls on mountain peaks.

But I've also tried to bring them parts of New China, thing like pop music from Pu Shu and Jay Chou, movies from directors Jia Zhangke and Wang Xiaoshuai — oh, and some random knickknacks, such as coupon booklets from McDonald's and Chinese-language newspapers.

Unfortunately, these "New China" gifts aren't usually a hit. Friends and family seem to prefer gifts from the China of old.

Once, while screening a DVD of Wang Xiaoshuai's *Beijing Bicycle* for my family, I proudly pointed out Beijing landmarks and offered (perhaps a little too much) insight into city life.

Soon, however, yawns and hunger began to overtake the whole family. Everyone took turns going to the refrigerator. Mom started ironing and folding clothes. Dad fell asleep. Only my brother remained. He insisted on sitting through the whole movie, but I knew deep down that he'd rather have been running up the score on some hapless team in his Xbox football game.

Over time, I've learned that my friends and family prefer to see *hutong* — not high-rises. They want to hear traditional folk music — not a Chinese Usher. And when I hand over the newspapers and McDonald's coupons, well, their puzzled look says it all.

"What am I going to do with this?"

Good question.

From what I can tell, gifts from China are meant to be shown off to anyone who comes within range. Get too close and a silent alarm will sound, prompting my mom to say: "Oh, that — Charlie brought it home from China. Isn't it beautiful?"

She could be talking about the scroll painting of the sparrow on a pear tree branch. Or she could be talking about the jade frog sitting on her desk at school — or about the neat miniature umbrella that opens to reveal the logo for the 2008 Beijing Olympics.

These gifts are conversation starters — conversations that end soon after they begin.

What else is there to say? Traditional, touristy gifts likes these confirm general information given, and assumptions about, China. For the average person, this is enough.

In giving gifts, I hope to buy permission to talk people's ears off about China — not just about the things they already know but also about the things I want them to know. That taxi drivers are some of the coolest Chinese people I've met. That waking up on the other side of the world can be terribly lonely and also unbelievably exciting.

Sometimes, my friends and family are gracious enough to give me a few minutes, but more often I'm left to answer the "So how's China?" question in 10 seconds or less.

In such cases, I just let the scroll paintings and Great Wall T-shirts speak for themselves.

CHARLIE SHIFFLETT

(July 12, 2007)

7. THE FUNNY THING IS

88. Jokes are a funny way to learn

My Chinese language teacher was in hysterics after finally understanding the meaning of an unusual colloquial English phrase.

Her previous student, my Aussie mate Ben, had written the colorful phrase on the whiteboard, and told teacher Ding that I would translate before class began.

The statement read: "I could eat the crotch out of a low flying duck." It was lunchtime and Ben was obviously very hungry.

For the next few minutes, the teacher and I discussed the different aspects of the expression, however, she was continually puzzled to find the humor.

Why was it a duck? Why was it low flying? And what is a crotch? All the elements of the joke were explained and none made any sense to my curious friend. "Why was this a funny expression?" she asked.

Her rationale was fair enough. Ducks are delicious, they sometimes fly low to the ground, and the genital areas of many animals are popular dishes for some in China.

The tide of understanding turned when she finally understood that Ben was so hungry he would reach up to the sky and grab the foulest and dirtiest food he could lay his hands on, even if it tasted absolutely disgusting to him. I explained that Ben was so famished that he would even eat the duck's droppings.

To the teacher, big Ben's hunger was really funny, not the crotch of the low flying duck. The image of the former rugby player eating duck droppings was really funny.

The following language class was as challenging as ever, and it confirmed once again I have a lot to understand about the people of the Middle Kingdom and their ways.

If you ever hear one of those smarty expats boast about how learning Chinese is straightforward and basic, he or she is lying through their teeth.

Sentences are twisted, and there are hidden agendas everywhere. Chinese often give vague, indefinite and even evasive answers to direct questions.

"Where are you going? (*Ni qu nar?*)" can receive the usual vague reply: "I'm going nowhere (*Wo bu qu nar*)." If a nosy friend notices you carrying shopping bags and asks what you bought, you have every right to say "I bought nothing" even if you're also being followed by an Ikea truck and there are four workers unloading the 10-piece dining room suite into your apartment.

However, Chinese humor is universally funny. I'm learning characters, and after learning a new batch of words, I have to read an amusing story.

I'm a bit like teacher Ding and I don't laugh immediately, because I'm reading each word slowly like a 5-year-old and there is no flow. I don't get the punch line straight away but a few moments later, when I get it, there is always a smile on my dial.

The following is a typical joke. A guy goes into a late-night tavern and notices one fellow sitting alone and talking aloud to himself. This bleary-eyed bloke is laughing one moment and then looking angry the next. He asks the gibberer about his odd behavior, and the drunk says: "I'm telling myself jokes ... when I hear a new one I laugh, but if I've heard it before, it really makes me angry."

PATRICK WHITELEY

(Oct 25, 2007)

89. Chinese know no humor

I was once invited to the taping of a TV show, and before the cameras started to roll, a young man came on stage and asked everyone in the audience to practice applauding.

At first, the applause was weak, but repeated efforts turned it into a thunderous ovation. It was as if everybody had just heard an important official's speech.

When I caught the show on air, our loud-applause practice session was added when the MC appeared.

I now understand that this off-screen cheerleader is a new species called the "Applause Leader". The need for his talent is understandable.

The Spring Festival Eve gala, known for being splashy, shallow and phony, probably gives more emphasis to the applause than to hosting.

This all leads me to question as to whether our joy is really heartfelt, and whether we Chinese really have a sense of humor.

When Ma Ji, the great standup comedian in the late 1970s and early 1980s, died a few weeks ago, I interviewed one of his colleagues. He said that when Ma got on stage, whatever he said made people laugh.

I studied the recordings of his gags. The audience was always grinning, even when Ma was not delivering the best punch lines. Maybe he looked funny, I thought, but gradually realized people of that era were always ready to burst into laughter because they had it inside them. It had little to do with how funny his routines were.

Before the "cultural revolution" (1966-76), I believe Chinese people harbored gratitude. People were happy, especially those in Beijing. After the downfall of the "Gang of Four", they regained their enthusiasm because they could again live a normal life. Standup comedy (or "cross-talk" in some parlance) tended to flourish after political turmoil ended.

During stretches of peace and prosperity, it was not as effective. This has nothing to do with the quality of the material or the delivery.

I have concluded that we Chinese do not have much of a sense of humor. If you're endowed with humor, you'll know what joy is. However, a joyous person may not know what humor is.

I've studied the speech patterns of Chinese people from all walks of life. They are invariably dry and devoid of humor. Former Premier Zhu Rongji has it, but he is one of a kind. Some folk artists have it, but most folk music dwells on misery and folktales are strong on peculiarity.

Everyone watches the televised gala for Zhao Benshan, the famed folk comedian. If he is absent, there would be twice as much mudslinging at the show.

Stephen Chow does not convey humor — just dramatic exaggeration. He is popular because people do not know real humor.

Hence, we have the word *gao xiao*, which implies the laughs are not from within but, rather, caused by outside stimulation.

The *Steamed Bun* is the only piece in 2006 that could sustain me. The others were nonsensical but still popular, proving we have nothing better to do.

What we Chinese people do have is wisdom, but this wisdom is not generously reflected in humor. We don't have many old joke books, but we have tons of books on duplicity, hypocrisy and infighting.

We don't have a strong demand for humor; we just want our karaoke.

WANG XIAOFENG
(Jan 17, 2007)

90. Why Chinese humor is so funny

I enjoy reading Hotpot columnist Wang Xiaofang's pertinent observations on modern Chinese society but yesterday my learned colleague made the bizarre claim that Chinese people do not have a sense of humor.

Wang, you've got to be kidding? Chinese are hilarious and have been making the world laugh for ages. One of the funniest books I have ever read was penned by a Chinese man 500 years ago. *Journey to the West* by Wu Cheng'en is a marvelous mix of folklore, allegory, religion, history and anti-bureaucratic satire.

The story is about a monkey who leads a monk, a pig and fish to India to retrieve Buddha's scrolls in an effort to find enlightenment. Monkey is a boastful genius who offends every monster or deity he meets. His standard greeting is: "I suppose you want to fight me, don't you?" Then he thrashes them senseless.

In the early 1980s, my brother and I watched the English version of the *Monkey* TV series every day after school. The ridiculous antics of this ancient Chinese comedy traveled through time and space and had us Aussie kids in stitches.

Pigsy was my brother's favorite. The porker only wanted to eat at banquets and chase pretty girls. For about a year, my brother and his little mates called themselves "Pigsy"!

I recently re-read the classic, and it's even funnier 25 years later.

When Monkey finally reaches India, Buddha's scroll keepers demand a bribe. Monkey refuses, so the corrupt officials give him blank paper. The pilgrims cannot understand why Buddha would employ such rogues.

"As a matter of fact," Buddha says to them, "blank scrolls such as these are the true scriptures." That Buddha always gets the best punch lines.

Fast forward 500 years and Stephen Chow's *Kung Fu Hustle* keeps the Chinese chuckles coming. His movie has magic, monsters and, just like *Monkey*, lots of nonsense, too. In one scene, Chow's sidekick throws butter knives at a crazy woman and the blunt blades keep bouncing off the walls and landing in Chow's body. It happens three times, and each time is funnier than the last. Simple gags are the best gags.

Wang claimed Chow's exaggerated style was an example of why the Chinese do not have much of a sense of humor (I'm presuming Wang is exempting himself from this sweeping generalization). It's kind of ironic, that someone such as Wang, who is renowned as an online funny guy, can be so damn serious and critical about everybody else's humor.

That's not very funny, Wang.

One fact we all know is that the Chinese sense of humor did not coincide with blogging. I'm sure Peking Man — who lived in the capital 400,000 years ago — chuckled when he saw his buddy slip on a banana peel.

Laughter is a timeless joy and is not limited by race or even age. A friend told me about his 8-year-old son's outrageous prank. He asked his boy to take a picture of something funny.

The boy ran away with a digital camera in hand and soon returned with a big grin. The cheeky boy had taken a picture of his bottom. Father and son looked at the picture and laughed themselves silly.

A sense of humor, my dear Wang, is a matter of opinion and to paraphrase Clint Eastwood, my favorite Hollywood comedian: "Opinions are like bottoms; everybody's got one."

PATRICK WHITELEY

(Jan 18, 2007)

8. THINK ABOUT IT

91. Ancient wisdom for modern life

I throw three coins.

They clink on the table and create a hexagram, and then I consult the *I Ching* (*Book of Changes*), as I have done for 15 years. The hexagram addresses what is really going on in my life, on all levels, not just the obvious ones. I count on it to guide me.

When this becomes known among my Chinese friends and students, they all declare that the *I Ching* is too difficult and too ancient to understand. To me, the *I Ching* is my constant source of guidance and the easiest thing in the world to comprehend. It applies to modern life as precisely as any book published today, at least in recent English translations.

The wisdom of the *I Ching* has come down from thousands of years of Chinese philosophical thought. It seems to have its deepest layers rooted in a time before Confucius. So how does this ancient Chinese oracular system relate to an American in today's society, to those dilemmas and lifestyles?

To me the answer is simple. Balance is the key in the *I Ching*. That was wisdom 3,000 years ago and is just as true today. Human nature has not changed much through time. All the modern self-help books try to help readers create balance in their stressful lives.

The way of the *I Ching* is to guide us to correct the world through correcting ourselves by thinking about events in a different way. The Buddha long ago stated that, "We are what we think". The *I Ching* counsels that it is not the events that happen in our lives that matter. It is how we think about them.

Through the *I Ching* we learn to rethink our frustrations, anger, disappointments and other strong emotions to our benefit. These are also the consistent messages of today's psychologists and even business gurus.

Master Oogway in *Kung Fu Panda* tells Panda Po: "Nothing is static. It is up to us to adjust." The *I Ching* reminds us that life ebbs and flows. And, with acceptance, we must go with, not against, it.

When I find myself caught up in emotions I quickly toss the coins and

Luo Jie

without fail, receive counsel on how to detach from them and let the world roll on.

The *I Ching* doesn't label events good or bad. It tells me that whatever happens, I can learn and benefit from it, and it gives me guidance on how to do that.

In *Kung Fu Panda*, Oogway tells Shifu: "There is just news. There is no good or bad news." What is not easy is accepting that all the events are opportunities for positive change.

For years, I was living a life filled with the heavy responsibilities of family, profession and trying to achieve The American Dream of prosperity. I was always trying to control this and that — to achieve more, to have more. All my hard work and good intentions only led to a life of endless acquisitions, exhaustion and a deadened interior.

I stopped trying to conform to the old ideas of what would make me happy. I heeded the wisdom of the Buddha, who said: "Peace comes from within. Do not seek it outside."

I wanted an entirely different approach to life.

Master Yoda said in *Star Wars*: "Either do it or don't do it. There is no try." So I stopped trying for happiness from external things, moved to live simply in Hawaii, ended up in China, and have been peaceful and happy ever since.

The *I Ching* neither preaches nor scolds, nor threatens. It simply points out the consequences of my choices. If I behave this way, this will be the result. If I behave that way, that will be the result. It's my choice.

Regardless of the century or the language, these basic truths prevail.

I never ask the *I Ching* a direct question. Instead, before I toss the coins I say: "Please tell me what I need to know today." And it always does.

SANDRA LEE
(June 17, 2009)

92. Waiting for the white rabbit

Chinese sayings are baffling to the untrained observer.

Back home in Australia, I had a friend who was obsessed with a racehorse called Little Red Dragon. He backed it at 60/1, and this flashy little filly won Jimmy a small fortune. But Little Red Dragon became Jimmy's curse. He always backed it and ended up losing more than five times the amount he initially won. "You're putting all your eggs in one basket," we warned.

In China they would say: "Jimmy, you are a farmer sitting near a tree stump waiting for a white rabbit." The saying is based on the story of a farmer who saw a rabbit kill itself by crashing into a tree stump. The farmer took the plump rabbit to market and was overjoyed by his small fortune. The old man walked back to the stump and waited for another white rabbit. By all accounts, he is still waiting.

This ancient saying is used today by 30-something Shanghai yuppies talking about a questionable stock rise. These guys, like many fortune hunters in the Middle Kingdom, are all trying to pull rabbits out of their hats, trying to conjure up some magic in a bid to get rich quick.

But we know it's all folly. Vanity, vanity, vanity, all is vanity, said the philosopher. What shall a man profit if he gains the whole world but loses his soul?

I love the odd idiom, but whenever I mention a famous saying, such as the above Biblical references or even Greek words of wisdom (know thyself is gem), there are Chinese idioms that say a similar thing.

This is no coincidence, and after doing extensive research I would like to share a theory.

I believe there was a period in history in which a group of really wise people got together and made up every wise saying there ever was. They then handed them out, and we're still saying them today. The philosophy fest happened about 500 BC.

Confucius (551-479 BC) gave birth to a school of thought followed by more people for more generations than any other human being in history. But all his wise sayings interestingly corresponded with the philosophical flourishing in the West via Socrates (469-399 BC) and his fellow Greeks. There was also a fine fellow called Siddartha Gautama (563-460 BC) who came up with some damn good ideas about living a happy life. Most of us know him as Buddha.

So I reckon something happened before these guys got all fired up. Maybe space ships visited earth and a bunch of really smart aliens told everybody how it all worked. Maybe about 500 BC, humans reached their spiritual zenith and discovered the true meaning of this funny thing called life.

I was quite rattled by my sudden burst of enlightenment and searched for the world's best saying. I consulted wise people, meditated on mountains and even did a little chanting. However, the answer came from a Beijing bicycle repairman called Wang Xiao.

He was fixing my friend's bike, and I asked the repairman for the world's best saying. Wang fixed the broken wheel, spun it back to health and handed the bicycle back to my friend. He then smiled at me.

"Be nice."

PATRICK WHITELEY

(Aug 14, 2007)

93. Lessons from the old wise guys

A group of starry-eyed men gathered on a mountaintop to listen to the man in a flowing robe.

The afternoon light danced on the teacher's beard, and the pilgrims could see their master's aura. Love one another and you will be of great benefit to the world, he told them. This was his answer to life, the universe and everything.

Good old Mo Zi (470-391 BC) was one of the many philosophers who triggered an explosion of ideas, which laid the foundations for today's Chinese psyche. The Hundred Schools of Thought period emerged during an era of great upheaval in Chinese history, which I have been overdosing on over the past week.

I love the golden week holidays. It is always a time for long lunches, relaxing afternoons with friends and a little reading. And when it comes to Chinese history, too much reading is not enough.

I discovered that for more than 450 years, seven major states battled to rule the Middle Kingdom and rivers of blood flowed as the sovereigns adopted different strategies to conquer one another. Although the Spring and Autumn, and Warring States periods (770-221 BC) were scarred by civil unrest, it also was an unprecedented era of cultural prosperity.

Today, China is enjoying a similarly prosperous time, so I thought I would spend the recent holidays thinking up a school of thought I could embrace. I started with

Confucius (551-479 BC), who has been followed by numerous people for generations.

But the school of thought that impressed me the most was the ideas of Mo Zi. He opposed Confucius and his emphasis on ritual, regarded warfare as wasteful and advocated pacifism. He called for a universal love encompassing all human beings in equal degree. Non-aggression was the key, which was an interesting concept in an era called the Warring States.

In developing my own school of thought, I kept reading Chinese history, looking for clues. As well as Mohism and Confucianism, there was Taoism, Legalism, *Yin-Yang* School, Logicians, Strategists, Legalists and the Eclectics.

One of the founders of the Taoist school was Lao Zi, who developed the Way — an absolute, overriding spirit transcending time, space and the whole universe. He advocated doing nothing and believed in letting events take their own course. I really like this idea about doing nothing.

The school of *yin-yang* and the five elements explained the universe in terms of basic forces in nature, the complementary agents of *yin* (dark, cold, female, negative) and *yang* (light, hot, male, positive) and the five elements (water, fire, wood, metal and earth).

The Logicians were represented by Sun Long, who wrote a book called *Gongsunlongzi*, which reflected his art of elegance. He took ideas from everybody, just like me.

All these thinkers were an eclectic bunch, and, funnily enough, there was even a group who called themselves the Eclectics. A key theme of all these schools of thought was importance of learning from history, which is a little overwhelming here in China. The more I learn about China, the more confused I become.

So, I guess that makes me a Confusionist, which isn't so bad, because I can confidently answer every question with: "I don't know."

PATRICK WHITELEY

(Oct 9, 2007)

94. Stories that pack a powerful punch

It unleashes enough internal energy to dispel a legion. It bulldozes foes with a frightening force. Those foolish enough to stand in the way risk having their innards mashed.

Roaarrrrrrrr!

This is the Dragon-Subduing 18 Palms, one of the most powerful kungfu techniques in the Chinese martial arts universe and a skill I have dreamed of acquiring since I was young.

The 18 Palms is just one legendary move to fulfill my kungfu fantasy.

There is the Six Meridian Mystic Swords skill; this allows the user to harness his internal strength and channel it through his fingers, which become deadly power beams that pierce through enemies.

Or consider the Universal Shifting Stance, which redirects and reverses opponents' attacks through uncanny manipulation of energy streams within the body. Maybe even the Toad Technique, which uses absorbed poison to increase internal energy for lethal blows.

OK, all of these might sound baffling or even downright ridiculous, especially the last example.

But therein lies my point. It is nearly impossible to appreciate these imaginary kungfu skills in English on their own because a large chunk of the cultural and literary connotations are lost in translation.

Those who persist in understanding these pillars of the Chinese martial literary tradition, or *wuxia*, might want to start by watching the numerous TV serials and screen editions of Louis Cha's 15 seminal works. Through these, they can see how the 85-year-old author continues to delight generations of Chinese at home and abroad with his fighting feats.

Cha himself is one of the best-selling Chinese authors of all time. More than 100 million copies of his works have been translated into multiple languages since he churned out his first *wuxia* series in newspapers in 1955.

Listen carefully to what a Beijing cabbie is tuning in to the next time you are in the capital. You might wonder how your driver gets blissfully lost in the *wuxia* world read out on the radio waves, soothing him as he navigates the capital's congestion.

Catching up on the *wuxia* background might also help audiences in the West better savor surreal takes on the genre, such as *Ashes of Time Redux*, the latest offering by auteur Wong Kar-wai. The movie is actually a reedited version of his 1994 piece.

Still, anyone can identify with the *wuxia* world's timeless themes of a hero's code of honor, courage and social justice.

Read into Cha's novels, like *Demi-gods and Semi-devils* or *Heavenly Sword and Dragon Saber*, and you might also find the foremost ingredient in any successful story — the one that transcends language and culture — is true love.

Yes, for all the gravity-defying, boulder-smashing and bone-crushing duels among the best *wuxia* warriors, the top pugilistic prize often involves getting the girl.

Do these subjects sound familiar? They should, because they also appear in classical novels like *Romance of the Three Kingdoms* and *Outlaws of the Marsh*, works that any expert on China worth his salt will say is essential

reading for those who want to understand this country.

For now, I'm happy delving into the mysteries behind one of the most elusive *wuxia* manuals — the Jiuyang Shengong treatise on ultimate inner strength — and maybe even learning a thing or two from it.

ALEXIS HOOI
(April 7, 2009)

95. Hugging the boundaries of personal space

On a flight to Europe last summer, I was seated between two middle-aged Chinese men.

The man in the aisle seat didn't make eye contact, get up or in any way acknowledge my existence, nor did the man in the window seat. They both sat with arms folded, staring straight ahead.

To get to my seat, I climbed over the legs of the first one. And as I did so, my bag flew out of my hands and landed in the other guy's lap. I was desperately trying to apologize, but neither would so much as glance at me!

The 14-hour flight was off to the worst possible start, and I was terribly embarrassed.

Traveling on a bus or train in China, I've experienced a similar personal space puzzle. Most travelers choose the aisle seat and, as the vehicle fills up, will not move to the window seat. Instead, the next person has to climb over the legs of the first passenger who is often oblivious to the problem since there is no eye contact or communication.

According to the experts, I'm sensitive to this because as an American I require more personal space and eye contact than any other group. This may well be so, because it took me a long time to get used to situations where close public body contact was the norm, not the exception. We even have a saying to describe someone who is too close or too angry to stay the "appropriate" distance away. We say they are "in my face".

When queuing, I notice that many Chinese are comfortable right up against the people in front and behind. Glaring doesn't seem to get me anywhere in these circumstances, and I'm sure people wonder what my problem is, as I try to make some space around me.

The study of personal space is called proxemics, a term coined by anthropologist Edward T. Hall. Studying what is one's comfort zone, he concluded that I need at least 1.2-2.1 meters between me and an acquaintance, but good friends can come within 45-75 cm.

Here's the variable: I'm a hugger. In Hawaii, I fit right in. Everyone hugs everyone else all the time.

In my birthplace, New England, where showing emotions is suspect behavior, I am a distinct nuisance. One of my sisters noticeably braces herself when we meet. She murmurs, "just one hug", as she endures my need to make that contact.

In China, if I forget where I am and hug someone on meeting them, they usually freeze and simply don't know how to react to such an aberration of acceptable behavior. We are both embarrassed. Some of my Chinese friends have come to accept my hugs, but some have not.

A term called "spatial empathy" was first coined by foreigners in Hong Kong, who had great difficulty adjusting to being in close bodily contact with others in the incredibly crowded streets, markets and office buildings.

It's pretty amusing to think of those Brits and Europeans trying to navigate the narrow alleyways of old Hong Kong without touching anyone — and having all and sundry staring at them and laughing. Foreigners considered staring yet another invasion of their precious private space. Being laughed at must have ruffled their dignity.

In truth, we are all creatures of habit. Our most ingrained habits we call culture. What feels right to me feels wrong to you.

Space, or lack of it, has a huge arc of what feels "normal" around the world. Sometimes, though, the logic is hard to identify. I don't like to be pressed up against in a line or a crowd, but, on the other hand, I can easily hug strangers.

I don't think even proxemics can find an easy label for that!

SANDRA LEE
(April 15, 2009)

9. A CLASS OF THEIR OWN

96. My meter-high bilingual master

Bringing up a child in a foreign land has many advantages. To me, the major one is that he or she will grow up learning another language without trying to.

My child was born here, and at nearly 4 years old, speaks Chinese and English equally well. His Chinese is of course far better than mine, his tones are spot on and he has no trace of a foreign accent.

Feeling slightly envious of this, and while I still have the chance to stamp my authority on him, I find myself constantly reminding him that my English is still better than his.

At the moment, my Chinese is up to understanding more or less everything he says, even the swear words he is already coming back from kindergarten shouting out to startled, kindly neighbors as we walk down the street.

But what I hadn't bargained for was a shift in the balance of power that comes with the ability to not just speak the language but to speak it like a native.

In the depths of winter it's cold walking back from school. One afternoon, we stopped to speak to a neighbor I'd known since I was pregnant. She was with her toddler.

No sooner had we stopped to say hello than the conversation was simply snatched out of my mouth.

"Boy or girl?" piped up my 4-year-old.

"Boy."

"Nice and fat, isn't he? I should think he eats well. How old is he now? How's he sleeping?"

And so the conversation went on, from general chitchat about her son's well-being, to my own son's school, the food he eats there, the teachers and so on.

After 10 minutes on the sidelines stamping my feet with the cold, I heard myself whine: "I'm freezing. Can we go home now?"

"In a minute, I'm just talking," chided my meter-high master.

A week later, I picked him up on my bike. We passed a classmate of his, who is collected every day by her grandparents. On this particular day, Granddad had been too busy to come, so it was just Grandma.

I was just about to call out to the little girl, "See you tomorrow!" when a voice rang out from the child seat behind.

"Her grandfather hasn't come to pick her up today then?"

He didn't address his own peer. It was Grandma he spoke to, who simply answered: "No, he hasn't come today."

The incredible thing about this, to me, was the way he knew exactly how a Chinese greeting would be made. It would not have occurred to me to say it, although stating the obvious is often a polite form of greeting, for example, "Come back then?" when it's obvious you have just returned home.

My 4-year-old knows this better than me, someone who has lived in China for twice the length of his lifespan.

Last week, a toothless old man smiled at him in a park.

"What happened to your teeth?" piped up my little boy.

"Oh, they just fell out," the old man said, with no trace of embarrassment or offence.

If a Western child had said that to an old Western man, his mother would have scolded him furiously for being rude. But on this occasion, my son had already worked out that as he, a little boy, meant no offence, the old man wouldn't take any.

This ability to communicate completely naturally is something I will never have as a learner of Chinese, no matter how perfect my tones become or how flawless my grammar.

I started feeling quite grumpy about this talent as we reached the door of our home. Then, suddenly: "Mummy, I can't open the door, and I'm hungry, and I want some milk, and I'm tired. Can I have a lollipop?"

Thank goodness. At least between us, I still have the power.

DEBBIE MASON

(March 25, 2009)

97. Life with ducks, chickens and woodpeckers

"Have you seen my daughter?"

I detect a slight anxiety in the voice of the mother. She is wearing a casual pair of blue jeans and a tight, woolen cardigan, just right for the warm spring weather.

"Don't worry, Monica, your girl is safe in this village. There are no roads around our inn and the locals are very friendly."

Her eyes are beautiful, proud and green. She smiles. From mother to mother. No more words are needed. We go to look for her daughter together.

Twenty months ago, we moved from Switzerland to the small village of Chaolong near Yangshuo, Guangxi Zhuang autonomous region, to run the Outside Inn, a 26-room countryside retreat.

And life has been good to us. I home-teach our 9- and 7-year-old sons, which leaves them plenty of time to have the kind of childhood my mother used to tell me about when reminiscing about her early years.

We walk through the gardens over to the pomelo orchard.

Desmond is calling down to me from high up his favorite climbing tree. "Are you all right, Mommy?"

I ask him if he has seen the little girl in the pink jumper with the picture of Minnie Mouse on it. Yes, she might have gone down to near the ping-pong table.

Once more, I notice the absence of street noise and city stress, and feel happy to have chosen this path.

Lenny is running past me with a mischievous smile. His trousers are covered in dirt — a real boy's trophy from his great day outdoors — and his fingernails are long like those of the village youth.

The 5-year-old son of a guest is right behind him. They are both holding a bamboo stick taken, no doubt, from the big bush by the entrance, and practice their kungfu skills.

One of our neighbors is stepping out from the toilet — not much more than a hole in the ground — in a simple, square and unfinished brick building, just like her house. The 40-year-old woman is getting ready for a day in the rice field.

Time to plant the seedlings for yet another harvest. She is wearing blue jeans and a non-descript, worn and loose-fitting top. A mobile phone is peeking out of her trousers' pocket.

She waves to me.

Her boy has befriended ours. Sometimes, after school, they play hide-and-seek together.

But he doesn't have much time. His lesson plans are tough and, recently, the language barrier has become a problem between the local children and ours. It seems that even though it has never mattered before, now, at their age, their friendship is in need of verbal communication.

She smiles, too. From mother to mother. And her eyes are beautiful, too.

Michael, my husband, is standing by the reception helping some American guests organize their day's activities. Yes, he has seen the girl with the Minnie Mouse jumper near the front. A Dutch family that lives and works in Shanghai is lazing in the hammocks, enjoying the peace of this island within a busy world.

The previous night they had seen stars for the first time in a long time.

Lulu, our sausage dog, comes running. Her thin tail is sticking up vertically, underlining her eagerness to go for a walk.

We take a right turn.

"Guten Morgen, Peter," I call to a guest from Germany and then "*Ni hao*" to the old lady from down the road, who is taking her two muddy water buffaloes to the fields.

Life is good, indeed.

As if in approval, a woodpecker gives a few loud pecks on the bamboo, some chickens flutter past and a cicada can be heard in the lush distance.

There she is, the little girl, beaming with happiness.

"Look, Mommy, a family of ducks has come to say, 'hello'!"

NADINE HUDSON
(June 3, 2009)

98. Double trouble for bicultural twins

Raising twins is complicated in any environment, but when they are raised in a multicultural home, the situation can sometimes get quite messy.

The first issue is how to address them.

Somewhere I read that it's best not to emphasize which twin is technically older.

Sibling rivalry is sometimes heightened among twins, and even the smallest edge can be something to fight about. Some parents withhold the information about who was born first from their children for years.

In our girls' first few days of life, I saw that this would not be a possibility for our family.

This disclosure is one of many ways that Chinese childrearing methods have taken hold in our North American home.

When they were born, my Chinese-born wife and her mother immediately began talking about "the big one" and "the little one". They meant age, not size.

Every Chinese person who visited wanted to know which one was big and which was little. They still do.

I don't think I've ever heard any of them ask how great the age difference

is. I used to volunteer that it was only a minute. They would nod politely —
and promptly continue with "big/little".

I've overheard some Chinese utterances that sound strange to my ear.

"The little one is actually bigger than the big one!" She certainly is
because she is quite an eater.

I don't know if it's just a way to refer to them, since older/younger is built
into the common Mandarin words for siblings or if the terms carry their full
weight, suggesting the older one deserves a bit of extra respect.

I know it's inevitable that they'll eventually start fighting over toys,
and the older one will probably think she should win because she's the "big
sister". Fortunately, I think I've figured out an appropriate response. I'll let
their mother handle it Chinese way, which she'll do as she does in dealing
with most of life's complexities.

To be fair, my wife has adapted to, and even embraced, American habits
on certain points.

For example, as we prepared to take the girls on a trip to China during
their early months, we figured they'd attract a lot of attention in public. And
we knew that well-intentioned Chinese people are quicker than Americans to
reach out to touch a cute baby.

But ours were born a few weeks premature, and we were afraid their
immune systems wouldn't be up to the challenge. We agreed to try to keep
strangers from holding or touching them.

The twins' mother performed admirably, even when she had to be rude.
When one smiling young woman leaned forward to grab a twin, she was left
with an armful of air — and a shocked expression on her face — as my wife
took two quick steps back.

But my wife doesn't buy into the American way of putting infants into
their own room with a baby monitor and pushing them to sleep through the
early night on. She figures that babies feel more secure sleeping in their

parents' room, and that they should develop their sleep habits in their own time.

She may be right. But ours still wake in the middle of the night, and that makes it hard in a nuclear family where both parents work full time.

And I've never been able to convince her that the twins should wear regular American pants instead of Chinese-style crotchless or cut-out ones. She and her mother have always sworn that these pants make diapers easier to change.

My attempts have probably been some of the funniest moments of raising twins in a bicultural home — and some of the messiest.

JAMES RITCHIE

(Sep 8, 2009)

99. **Fueling the fire of a tot's desire**

I was driving home one late afternoon when I saw a fire truck parked in our neighborhood.

It didn't alarm me, because there was a small child climbing up the ladder behind the truck. Two elderly people stood below, arms outstretched, to protect the toddler.

"What a naughty child," I thought.

But wait … wasn't that my very own 2-year-old?

My son has developed a new hobby. He loves shouting: "Fire (*zhao huo la*)!" and then waving his right arm at an imaginary target while calling out: "Ah Ge puts out the fire (*Ah Ge mie huo la*)!"

The Disney cartoon episode in which Mickey, Donald and Goofy put out a fire has become his favorite. Recently, he has come to love a domestically produced animation about a group of children who help firefighters. I thought the series was too complicated for him, but it seems my son has learned more than I expected.

Every night, he must hold a small fire truck model before going to sleep. One morning, he woke up asking for two fire trucks, but we only have one. My father suggested: "Ah Ge is the firemen's captain. I'll get you a special car to ride in." The little red racecar did the trick, and Ah Ge was quite happy with his promotion.

Firefighters in China have yet to gain the same kind of esteem they wield in the United States. But I find the masculine image a perfect idol for my boy, so I thought: Why not take him to meet these heroes in person?

When I finally found the fire station near our neighborhood, a young fireman was learning to drive a red truck, with an officer sitting beside him. Holding my boy high, I approached a guard.

"Excuse me, my son loves firefighters. Could we stay here watching you?"

The young man looked surprised, but when I told him more about my son's fascination, he seemed quite happy. He even ran to the officer and had a little discussion. To our surprise, he announced: "I'll show you around."

The door rolled up to reveal a bright red truck. "I drive this truck," our guide said with a big smile. Behind it was a car. Much to the delight of my son and father, that vehicle was reserved for the captain.

A side door opened and we found ourselves in an even bigger hall.

"This is our biggest fire truck, a Mercedes Benz imported from Germany!"

According to my untrained eyes though, all eight fire engines have received utmost care.

Pointing at the ceiling more than 10 m above us, our guide said: "We live up there and slide down the pole when the alarm rings."

Along the wall was a row of neatly folded uniforms, with a helmet atop each set. My father put one of the helmets on my son's head, and the fireman turned on the torchlight. The helmet was heavy, but the little fellow strived to stand straight.

As we waved goodbye, my son, who had up till now remained silent, raised his right hand to the forehead and cried out: "Salute (*jing li*)!"

LIU JUN
(April 19, 2007)

100. What's the rush, ent-boy?

My son has turned 4, but I'm increasingly impatient with him, believing he is too slow in almost everything. But sometimes I wonder, what's the hurry?

One morning, it was already 8 but my son was still playing with a toy car, while I waited for him to brush his teeth before rushing off to kindergarten.

"Hurry up! You are already late!" I couldn't help but raise my voice.

The boy reluctantly accepted my orders but spent more than one minute putting on his sandals. "You are just like the ent-child in *Lord of the Rings*," I joked.

Actually, J. R. R. Tolkien only talked about the ent, a slow-moving tree that takes care of the forest.

Jack Peterson made a funny, vivid portrayal of Treebeard the ent in his movie. But I'm more impressed by Tolkien's description of the ent-wives, who have left the ents to take care of their flower gardens.

When Treebeard said farewell to Merry and Pippin, he asked the hobbits to keep an eye on the ent-wives and the ent-children. Well, it seems one such ent-child is right in front of me.

My son enjoys the idea of ent-children very much, and we talked and moved in ent fashion all the way to school. "Gooooodbye!" I waved at him.

For the first time in many weeks, I didn't find myself enraged about his slowness.

It's interesting to realize that while my son was a toddler, we always told him to, "Slow down! Be careful!" We were afraid to let him explore his surroundings by himself, lest harm would befall the innocent child.

When did we begin to press him to speed up? And why the change of mindset?

Perhaps the change came after we were invited to the kindergarten several times to see how the children performed in class. I was annoyed because my son reacted much slower to the teachers' instructions than the few smart-seeming kids.

While the "top" students yelled out every Chinese and English word the teachers showed on cards, my son didn't seem to have a clue and wasn't very interested in the repetitive teaching method.

Although I know every person is different in ability, I couldn't help but become upset at thinking my son hadn't excelled.

I compared him to other children in more aspects and jumped to the conclusion that my son will miss his chance to rise above the rest.

But a thought struck me after making the ent joke. What's the point of all this hurrying around? Suppose we live to 100 years old. That gives us some 3.15 billion seconds to breathe, eat, sleep, laugh, cry and do whatever else makes a human life complete.

Do I want to turn myself into an alarm clock and make a good part of my son's early life unhappy?

The invention of modern technology has sped up our lives in an incredible way. The best place to feel this acceleration is in literature and film.

When I spent months reading *Lord of the Rings*, I often wondered at Tolkien's sense of time. It took Treebeard week after week to drum up other ents to fight Saruman, the bad wizard. But Jackson shortened the process to a matter of several scenes.

The same happened with the Trojan War, which lasted 10 years in Homer's epics but was finished in a few days in the Hollywood blockbuster.

In our hurry to finish the stories, we have to delete countless details that should have made the tales wonderful. In our hurry to reach our next life goals, we have developed tunnel vision and turn a blind eye to the beautiful scenery along the way.

With this revelation, I have gained more confidence in not pressing my son to memorize the abstract written characters but to instead encourage him to climb the trees and rocks and befriend strangers we meet.

By living as ent-wife and ent-child that Treebeard so longed for, I am finally happy with my son.

LIU JUN
(May 19, 2009)

EPILOGUE

101. Trapped in the revolving door

Round and round they go, in and out: China is a revolving door for most foreigners.

In just a little more than two years, I've seen scads of expats come and go and have attended more going-away parties than birthday bashes with them.

Another fresh batch of global nomads has recently appeared in Beijing, so I'm doing another round of meet-and-greets. One of the first things they ask after introductions is when I plan on returning to the United States. Most are surprised when I tell them I don't.

Like most other foreigners, when I first came to the country, I had planned on doing "my year in China" — a pit stop for adventure and experience on the journey to life's next destination.

But when that year ended, I wasn't ready to go. Some time ago, I came to realize I might never be, that perhaps when I stepped off that plane I was unknowingly stepping through a trap door rather than a revolving one.

China is a place of superlatives, where the suffixes "ist" and "est" apply to nearly everything, and the country's sheer extremeness either blurs or erases the line between hyperbole and understatement.

Beijing offers a particular appeal. The metropolis seethes with energy, and I would now find it difficult to feel so alive anywhere less sizzling. The capital changes so rapidly that I don't even have to move to live in a different city every year.

Also, China is a place where you should always expect the unexpected — and do so when you least expect it. And you can't expect the expected, especially when you most expect it. It's bewildering, paradoxical and oh so delightful.

The longer I live here, the more I understand the country — and the more I realize I don't. I knew China much better after my first three months than after my first year. Now, I'm afraid of how ignorant I will become 10 years on, when I will probably know 10 times what I do now.

All of these are ways in which the country has captivated my attention. But it's the people who live here that have captivated my heart, locking the revolving door and throwing away the key.

I have learned so much from the way people here treat one another — that is, with a veneration for cooperation, harmony and the collective good that bears little semblance to what I knew in the United States. And I have so much more to learn.

People often ask if I consider China home. I still don't know how to answer that.

But perhaps I could say the United States is my homeland and China is the land that has become my home. However, it will never be home to me in the same way it is to the Chinese or how the United States was to me but could never be again.

Having undergone the personal transformation that comes with living here, I today feel equally comfortable and uncomfortable on either side of the ocean. My way of thinking has been influenced by both my host and home culture, and in some ways has become like neither.

In the end, I believe the old adage, "home is where the heart is". I feel

that way about the United States.

But I also believe that the heart is where home is. And that's how I feel about China.

ERIK NILSSON
(Oct 22, 2008)